God and the Web of Creation

Ruth Page

SCM PRESS LTD

0 334 02653 9

First published 1996
by SCM Press Ltd
9–17 St Albans Place, London N I ONX

Typeset at The Spartan Press Ltd,
Lymington, Hants
and printed in Great Britain by
Biddles Ltd, Guildford and King's Lynn

God and the Web of Creation

To the memory of the late Margaret Peace, biology mistress at Tauranga Girls' College, in contrition for finding ecological wisdom bizarre and irrelevant in the 1960s;
and to the Society, Religion and Technology Project of the Church of Scotland, for converting me in the 1980s to the importance of ecological understanding for belief and practice

Contents

Introduction:

The Scope of the Study

In recent years perceptions of the world we live in have been shaped by two contrasting images. The first is of our blue-green planet travelling in space. From that came a new warmly appreciative perspective on its totality, for the entire planet became 'home'. The second image, on the other hand, is of interrelationship, which comes from a growing popular sense of how all the planet's creatures coexist and are interconnected, so that the whole in its entirety seen from space arises from the interaction, indeed the unconscious cooperation, of its parts. Both the large and the small scale changes of perception are caught and linked by Lewis Thomas:

> The most beautiful thing I have ever seen in a photograph, in all my life, is the planet Earth seen from the distance of the moon, hanging there in space, obviously alive. Although it seems at first glance to be made up of innumerable separate species of living things, on closer examination every one of its working parts, including us, is interdependently connected to all the other working parts.[1]

This positive vision of the whole Earth and the web of its contributing parts becomes even more precious as its fragility and contingency are realized. At the same time as its positive interdependence is seen, the disorder of the planet has also become evident, including the degree to which humanity's impact on the natural world is having bad effects as well as good. So the point of view from which this doctrine of creation is written arises most acutely from the concatenation of mismanagement and misfortune known in brief as the ecological crisis. The signs of that crisis, from the pollution of individual rivers and seas to the global scale of climate change, have often been rehearsed, and I do not intend to list them again here, although I shall refer to them from time to time.[2] What is important and different in this starting point for a doctrine of creation compared to earlier versions is the perception of the unity of the created world, whose components are in a critical mess largely of human making. There can be no theological complacency here. There is some substance, as I shall demonstrate, in the criticisms of Christian theology for having, at least, had nothing to offer to halt the exploitative practices which have contributed so much to the crisis, even though such criticisms have often been overstated.[3]

The ecological crisis has produced many kinds of problems for humanity. Some are primarily in the domain of the scientists, like discerning the process of global warming. Many have ethical overtones, such as the question of nuclear power, whose lethal waste is so difficult to dispose of safely. Other issues affect consumer life-styles in everything from buying organically grown vegetables to recycling bottles and cans. All such problems do impinge upon theology, which has all life under God in its sights, and offers values from Christian belief to give point to action. But two issues are made immediately pressing by the crisis which are peculiarly the responsi-bility of theology, while their implications will affect the doctrine of creation.

The first concerns *God's relationship with the natural world*. Celtic spirituality maintained a consciousness of the divine involved in all living, farming and fishing, as concerned as people were that all would be well. A prayer for the protection of cattle, for instance, begins:

> Pastures smooth, long and spreading,
> Grassy meadows beneath your feet,
> The friendship of God the Son to bring you home
> To the field of the fountains,
> Field of the fountains.[4]

There is a sense in these Celtic songs and prayers that everyone and everything – animals, fish, crops, peat fires, household goods, boats, weather, people, saints, angels and God – are all 'in this together' against the forces which would hurt or destroy.

The problems facing the planet now are far more intricate and more widespread than anything known in the Outer Hebrides when the Celtic prayers of the *Carmina Gadelica* were collected. It is not only the creatures of the household which are at risk, but wild creatures and even others not known to humanity. Chemical processes, economic and commercial practices, a population explosion with its attendant demands, all combine to produce problems of almost baffling complexity.

But increase in complexity does not remove the possibility of the basic vision where God is involved in all that goes on, valuing creation and desiring its good. What that means in theological terms will be a major part of this book. This close concern of God with creation, so that to see creation is also to see God-in-relation-with-creation, expresses more prosaically Edwin Muir's vision:

> Did our eyes
> From their foredestined watching place
> See Heaven and Earth one land, and range
> Therein through all of Time and Space?[5]

But this relationship must not be construed too prettily. Creation includes natural radioactivity, dinosaurs, tapeworms and the HIV virus as well as the more immediately humanly appealing panda or robin. Yet if the positive, caring nature of the divine relationship with every last creature is not seen as vital to a doctrine of creation, Christianity has nothing distinctive to bring to belief and action in the crisis. It is not enough simply to recommend Christian *human* activism, of the kind any concerned group might engage in, as if all present accounts of the connection between *God* and the *natural* world were adequate.

A doctrine of creation should have something to say about the way in which God is involved in, for instance, the processes of desertification. It may no longer be possible to believe that God will at one stroke, so to speak, step in and reverse the process, directly causing the desert to blossom as the rose. But on the other hand, we cannot believe that God is merely watching from a distance, or even is a distressed but helpless onlooker while humans are exhorted to get on with what has to be done. Yet that is the impression many books on Christian green stewardship give. The difficulties in speaking of God's active involvement cannot be denied; if it were simple, descriptions would abound. Yet in spite of the difficulties, which themselves must be described, something has to be said if God is to remain central.

If God is not understood to be in the thick of non-human suffering and the dangers to the planet, we simply continue the anthropocentricity Christianity is accused of, since that emphasis on human work will imply that God relates only to what humans do, then subsequently and secondarily, at a remove mediated by humanity, to non-human creation in its joys and sorrows. If that were the case, and it often seems to be presupposed, it implies that during all the aeons of evolution before humanity appeared there was no connection between God and creation. On the supposition that such a belief is untenable, quite apart from the ecological crisis of our own time, issues concerning the continuing relationship between God and all creation remain matters to be addressed.

If one of the consequences of the impact of the ecological crisis on theology is the insistence on God's presence in, and valuing of, creation, the other concerns *what, in the light of God's relation, is the relation of humans to non-human creation?* If God so values and cares for creation, how can humans treat it carelessly? That question again will be addressed later. But there is a further aspect of relationship with the natural world which must also be fully recognized. The poet Norman MacCaig expresses it thus:

> Such a web of likenesses. No matter
> how many times removed, I am cousin
> to volcanoes and leafbuds, and the heron
> devouring a frog eats a blood brother of
> suns and gravestones.[6]

Humans are part of this 'web of likenesses', and any theology which dwells only on the difference between human and non-human

(which in older theologies was often referred to as 'sub-human')
has missed an important element of the relationship which is
mutual. The metaphor of 'the web' is correct. Not only is a web a
pattern of interconnection, but when one part shakes, it all shakes.
Humans are not exempt from this vulnerability. Humanity's dependence on the natural elements of soil, water and air has been
shown up sharply in recent suffering from erosion, drought and
pollution. Human intelligence, technology and civilization may be
special marks of our species, and they have occupied theologians
for centuries. But our kinship with the rest of creation is equally
important. Once more, we are in this crisis together, and if we are
to get out of it, it will again be together.

The major Christian response to the ecological crisis has been to
dust down the notion of stewardship under God and make it play
what is undoubtedly an important role. It is far better to be a
steward than an exploiter, an indifferent onlooker, or merely a
consumer. Yet on its own that is not enough. It leaves humans in
their old dominating role managing the creation, 'humanizing' it, as
the process was once called. 'Management,' as Nigel Cooper notes,
and for that 'stewardship' may be read, 'assumes a culture of
control'.[7] Moreover, it leaves God inactive in relation to the natural
world, and at a distance from the creation where only humans are
engaged. Further, if there is no fellow-feeling with the rest of
God's creatures as all one creation, rather than a sense of
management superiority of humans over and apart from the natural
world, our stewardship will again run all the risks of unthinking
anthropocentricity.

I take unexamined anthropocentricity to be a bad thing, even
though I shall argue that some measure of human–centredness is
inescapable among humans. In the first place, stewardship could
foster human self-congratulation at the expense of the rest of
creation for being promoted to such responsibility under God.
Secondly, but more importantly, anthropocentricity diminishes
human comprehension of God by restricting conceptions of the
divine relationship with creation to those which may be expressed
in human, personal terms. 'Theologies of nature' may sometimes

be alert to the dangers, but doctrines of creation have been resolutely centred on the human.

What is needed now, therefore, is not another skirmish on the green fringes of belief but a rethinking of fundamental doctrine, almost as a matter of penance for what Christian doctrine has allowed humans to get away with. By the end I shall have described a theology with a generalized triangular shape, which has God, humanity and all the natural world at the three points, and lines of relationship running from each point in both directions. I believe that the possibility of these relations is what creation is about.

Such concern for the natural world, and regret at human complacency in past doctrine, do not exclude painful awareness of human degradation and poverty. The natural world is not the only one that suffers. The World Summit for Social Development in March 1995

> produced reams of sickening statistics. More than one billion people live in poverty around the world. Two billion do not have safe sanitation. Among people of working age 2.8 billion are unemployed. 20% of the world's population – the world's richest people – own almost 83% of the world's wealth; another 20% of people – the world's poorest – own only 1.4% of the world's wealth.[8]

And so one could go on, through statistics for malnutrition, street children, illiteracy, torture. Moreover:

> the five nations that are permanent members of the Security Council are responsible for more than 80% of arms traded internationally each year.

The mess the world is in, therefore, has human as well as non-human tragedy, the failure of relationships among humans as well as the failure to care about the natural world. But having acknowledged that, and although I shall make connections occasionally between human and non-human suffering, this book will dwell primarily on what it all means for belief concerning the natural world, since that has had less exclusive attention, and for a shorter time. I should say also, in these initial remarks, that although it is the 'travail of nature', a phrase Paul might recognize, with which I am largely concerned, there is much in the natural world to give joy and pleasure to humans, and an uninterrupted life to non-humans. It is because the good is very often possible that the bad becomes reprehensible.

Incidentally, I recognize that the phrase 'the natural world' is a misnomer used like this, since humans are also part of nature. But if it can be taken to refer to what is not human in creation, it saves always defining that part in terms of what it is not. While I am on the subject of language, I have to regret that many writers, even contemporary and recent writers, on matters of theology and ecology, are still using exclusively male terms. It is as if sensitivity on one issue precluded sensitivity on another.

Thus far I have described the actual trigger for writing this book as the questions raised by the ecological crisis. But for a rounded doctrine of creation to address all contemporary issues, quite another area of interest has to be addressed. Scientific cosmology, for the first time in many generations, seems to offer a possibility of Christian interpretation. Several optimistic accounts have appeared invoking new cosmic versions of the argument for God's existence from the design or order of the world. No book on creation could avoid the issues this raises, for one cannot neatly divide the subject, as if cosmology could be described as creation, while all the rest is to be treated separately, perhaps as providence. It is precisely part of the problem that the natural world has been treated only as providence for humanity, with no intrinsic value to God of its own as creation. Any doctrine of creation today, therefore, has to consider both cosmology and life on earth, in spite of the wide differences which now exist between the disciplines of physics and biology.

Issues raised by these sciences will have to be considered throughout. Moreover, the clash of perspectives between a physicist's view of 'the intelligibility of the world, its transparent rational harmony' on the one hand, and the flux and turmoil indicated by the ecological crisis on the other, has to be explored.[9] For that reason the first part of this book, although it will be concerned with the understanding of God and the world out of which the doctrine arises, will also have to address much more technical questions of what may constitute knowledge, design and critical realism, for these arise in the process.

Paying attention to what scientists say, even critical attention to how they say it, is one major cause of any contemporary doctrine of creation standing in a problematic relation to the Bible. One of the unresolved confusions in Brunner's version of the doctrine, for instance, comes from the difference between what he wishes to say from the Bible as interpreted from his neo-Orthodox perspective, and what he has taken from Bergson about evolution, which is, in fact, restricted to a separate section.[10]

Some parts of the Bible travel well, as they say of wines, to this new context, but more often as vision rather than as practice. Thus much has rightly been made of the attitude of care shown in the observance of the Sabbath and Jubilee rest for farm animals and the land within a covenanted relationship with God (Ex.23.12; Lev.25.1–7). But no one, as far as I know, is actually advocating its implementation as Sabbath observance, as opposed to a general concern for the well-being of farm animals.

There are thus hand-holds for current doctrine in Scripture, mainly in the Hebrew Scriptures. But Genesis 1, for instance, presents a contemporary with a confusing *mélange* of a few general principles which may still be affirmed, such as the goodness of matter (though that is a deduction from the text, at home in a context where spirit was prized over matter), bound up with impossible occurrences, such as the creation of all species, instantly, in six days. It is hard to be consistent in what one is doing in referring to the biblical texts, although such reference may seem reassuring. It is possible to have some sympathy with Ian Ball's trenchant comment.

> Viewed from outside it seems strange that the members of a major institution [the church] should feel so obliged to justify themselves by constant reference to the quasi-metaphysical speculations of a nomadic tribesman of the second millennium BC![11]

Ball's attribution of authorship may not be exact, but his point could certainly be argued in relation to Genesis 1 whenever the ancient text is invoked, for instance, in ways that simply ignore or oversimplify his history of evolution.

Doctrines of creation, for example, frequently hark back, at least metaphysically, to a golden age of harmony in nature, which was disrupted only by human sin. But there never was a golden age in a world that evolved over millennia. If the world had ever had the kind of harmony described in Genesis 1, or Psalm 104, the ecological crisis would be more swiftly put right, for it would involve only the easier task of restoration. But the crisis is happening in the *real* world of interacting ecosystems, and their stresses, where order is temporary and contingent. It is God's relation to *that* world which has to be discerned.

Again, the straightforward traditional allocation of all evil to an origin in human sin will hardly do, real though that sin is. Within the vast time-scale of life on earth humanity has only just arrived. But all manner of suffering had been going on long before. A doctrine of creation ought to be concerned with such non-human suffering, and to be able to give some theological account of, for instance, why the dinosaurs became extinct.

Yet every Christian's belief has been shaped by the Bible generally, and is in some kind of lineage from some kind of understanding of the text. I shall wrestle with this question again when I come to discuss 'dominion' in Genesis 1, but for the moment this may serve to give notice that I believe the Bible to be too varied in what it says on creation, and in many places too far from what is taken for granted in contemporary society, for there to be a 'biblical' doctrine of creation which does not exercise severe selectivity and the fudging of issues.

Many of the matters I have been rehearsing in this introduction acknowledge the role of contingency within the created world. A world with contingencies is not fixed, but has a continual stream of *possibilities* being acted on in ways which may help or hinder creatures. I believe that the importance of possibility has been overlooked in theology. We have concentrated on the *res gestae*, the things done, or written, or thought, without dwelling on the range of possibilities out of which these *res* came. The existence of various possibilities in interpretation is increasingly noticed in modern theology, but that is only one aspect of the possibility of possibility with which we are surrounded. 'The possible' has been given less value than what has been held to be 'the actual', yet possibilities *are* valuable, and the fact that possibilities are possible is valuable. This version of the doctrine of creation celebrates possibility, and begins by exploring God's act in creation as the gift of possibility.

In brief, then, this book begins by arguing that what God created was possibility, a far more important characteristic of the world than has ever been acknowledged. In Part One that starting point leads both to a theological development concerning God letting possibility be, with creation responding by coming into being, and to the philosophical questions which cannot be avoided. Cause and effect, for instance, has been a combination explored in relation to actualities, but what meaning can it have in relation to possibility? That in turn raises the issue of whether God may be said to have 'caused' creation. At this point, as in others, modern scientific discussions enter in, with the claim often made that God caused the Big Bang with the whole future of the universe inherent in it. Again, with possibility in view, what remains of the categories of determinism and indeterminism? Is there a median between a totally fixed and a totally fluid world? And finally there lurks always the inescapable philosophical question: 'How do you know?'

Such questions and argument in Part One may seem abstract, and perhaps irrelevant, to those concerned primarily with God and the natural world, which becomes the chief concern from Part Two onwards. Yet, if the proposals of theology are to be more than an undefended statement of belief, they must be examined. The discussion of them, however, does not imply the kind of natural theology which argued from a state of affairs in the world to the existence of God. Such arguments can never be conclusive, and they generally depend on a very narrow selection of 'evidence'. Instead of that, what is implied in taking philosophical and scientific questions seriously is that *belief in God as creator, and experience of the world, should be able to be held together, so that belief about God gives point to experience, rather than contradicting, or being irrelevant to, it.* This is neither a Barthian exercise, with God as the only avowed starting point, nor a Schleiermacherian exercise beginning from experience alone (if, indeed, such descriptions are fair to these writers). It is an endeavour to keep belief, knowledge, experience and action together.

The whole of Part One, however, is only the beginning, and is in many ways a prologue to the consideration of life in the later sections. What may have seemed a minimal account of creation, with God freely creating possibility while creatures were free to use it as they could, is here broadened and deepened. The freedom of God and creation is then seen to be the condition which makes love and relationship possible, while divine love is worked out within the actualities and continuing possibilities of life in this world. It is possible for God and creation to work together in relationship, and the Christian basis for this vision of what creation is about comes from the Gospels' portrayal of the love used in freedom by Jesus in relationship with his Father.

When all the theological framework is in place, it can be seen that *all* creation, including the natural world humanity has been so free with, and has given so little theological importance to, is by its very being a response to the divine gift of possibility. Each creature lives in God's presence, and has its own relationship with God, to whom it is all valuable and intimately known. Only after that realization may questions of human ethical conduct arise. The book then closes with a kaleidoscopic vision of eternity, in which *all* that has pleased God, human and non-human alike, is gathered like a harvest from the whole web of creation.

Part One

Creation as Possibility and Freedom

1. Possibilities and the ultimate question of life

Actualities, the stuff of what happens, what is said, or done, however they are interpreted, are the staple of the understanding of life. Possibilities are much more marginal. A historian, for instance, may pause to consider the possibilities open to her protagonist before giving an account of what happened, and a scientific researcher may at least once describe failed possibilities before giving the successful method. But the things which are held finally to matter are what was done, and what worked.

Yet when the living of life is involved, rather than the giving of a consequential, communicable narrative, its fluidity and continuous possibilities are much more apparent. A. N. Wilson has a character in one of his novels reflect on this (although a novel is itself a 'consequential, communicable narrative'):

> Yet, while obviously true in one way, it is surely false that people can be got right or wrong, like mathematical puzzles, rather than being entities in a state of endless flux who react so differently to each separate combination of circumstances or relationships that it makes no sense to define them. It is upon the fallacy of fixed personalities that biographers have made their trade . . . The real me, and the real Hunter, as opposed to these mythological projections, were figures of infinite fluidity, and even as they sat together . . . they were many persons, possessed of many thoughts and aims.[1]

This kind of fluidity of being, however, could not take place unless the world at large were equally capable of change. It is from such possibility that streams of actuality flow, and are changed. Reality, therefore, is not necessarily hard-edged, agreed actuality; it can also be seen as a flow in which humans, and indeed all creatures after their kind, find themselves.

Thus, although life and work (including this book) have to be tidied up into what is comprehensible and communicable, life is lived and work done through a continuum of possibilities, sometimes many, sometimes few, some more weighted, more likely than others. In a sense possibilities are options for choice, but the choices of others, and possibilities as uncontrollable as the weather, may impinge upon the chooser, while not all options may be pursued simultaneously. Indeed at times the choice of one path excludes others for ever. On the other hand, even when the structure of a day is given – in a highly organized business, say – it is given only because earlier decisions among possibilities have already shaped it into a certain structure, and there remain possibilities of a variety of action, or varieties of ways in which an action may be carried out. It is a basic truism, though not one which receives much attention, that something must have been possible for it to have become actual.

An implication of human ease with actualities is that they are regarded as 'real', while only the possibility most foreseeable as future actuality is given that accolade ('a real possibility'). Reality is a term with its own difficulties, to which I shall return in considering critical realism, but it is, among other things, an expression of value. Thus what exists, what is done, what is actually said, has value, but what is possible has no value unless it can be seen to be about to impact the real. To some extent that is understandable; the possibility of my flying to China tomorrow does not command much attention. But a consistent valuing of the actual over the possible is limiting and bound to disappointment in a fluid multiple world.

Contrary to all of that, I wish to argue that the very existence of possibility is the most valuable thing in the world, for without it actualities would not have come into being, or could not be changed once they had arrived. The condition of possibility is logically and ontologically prior to actuality and has an irrefragable claim to be included in a sense of the real. Actualities exist only because they were, and continue to be, possible. Further, to think of the world only in terms of what happens and what exists is a short way with experience, if not a distorted view, precisely because the presence and effects of a wealth of possibilities are ignored.

This emphasis on a matrix of possibilities has important consequences for a doctrine of creation, since it has always been held that God created real, actual creatures. Such affirmation may have changed in its conception of God's *making* from the Genesis accounts, but still maintains the primary importance, for guiding general belief, of 'the things that are made', to use Paul's phrase from Rom.1.20. For a variety of reasons which will become clear in this book, and run from the problem of evil to the history of evolution, I find such an affirmation of God's creative action difficult to make in that way. But to say that God made it possible for there to be anything at all, rather than 'making' or 'designing' what is, allows for the contingent better and worse uses of possibilities by creation as it comes into being, flourishes and dies. One of the themes of this part of the argument is that such a conception allows for the *freedom* of both God and creation even while they remain related.

The difference made by moving conceptions of creation from actualities to possibilities can be shown by a change in what has often been called the ultimate question – the most basic question about the world. That has been formulated as: 'Why is there something rather than nothing?' That expresses a wonder that anything should *be* at all, and prompts the attribution of that 'something' to God. There may be difficulties in perceiving the hand of God in particular things, or their combination, as Blake, contemplating a tiger, wondered: 'Did he who made the lamb make thee?', but the amazing fact of reality/actuality remains.

In this case, however, ultimacy is bought at a price, and is in the last analysis questionable. The price comes in the abstraction of 'something' from actual creatures in their various lives, including the co-existence on one planet of tigers and lambs. Even if one is prompted to the answer 'God', such a God is extremely remote from instances of actuality. Again, the dubiety in fixing on 'Why is there something rather than nothing?' as the ultimate metaphysical question leading to a theological answer lies in separating off a pure fact of a total 'something' from all the impure, changing somethings which go to make it up. It is only the planet seen from space, and not its web of creatures. Granted a whole may be more than the sum of its parts, but a whole, a 'something' cannot be itself without its parts. And if the parts manifest moral and natural evil, as this world certainly does, that cannot be ignored in rising to an abstruse 'something'.

The ultimate question became important when theology could no longer answer proximate questions about the nature of the world. These were surrendered to the scientists while theology took an overarching teleological view, explaining why the world discovered by the scientists was there at all. That took theology off the defensive, indeed beyond disagreements and changes in the sciences, but, as already argued, at the price of disconnection with how things are.

The ecological crisis is one urgent contemporary instance of the way 'how things are' cannot in the end be ignored. As with human suffering, it raises proximate questions for which wonder at the existence of 'something' has always been inadequate. Yet proximate questions without an overarching sense of 'why?' cannot be answered adequately either. There is a need for a metaphysical background, but it has to be capable of connection with the ambiguous foreground.

For these reasons I propose that the metaphysical question to which theists find God to be the answer is: 'Why is anything at all possible?' That has advantages over the earlier formulation. First, the sense of wonder remains, but is redirected from a 'something' to the whole changing variety of what has been and now is in the world. What made all that possible? Secondly, the question concerning possibility rather than actuality retains the freedom of God as the giver of possibility, while also maintaining the freedom of creation in using it. That finite use of freedom in turn accounts for the possibility of moral and natural evil in the world – a matter I discuss at much greater length later.

It could be said with justice that a God who grants possibility for anything at all to be is as remote as the God responsible for something rather than nothing. But in this case possibility is the indispensable prelude to the relationship between God and the web of creation which grew from this freedom. The relationships are not those between maker and made, like a carver with a statue or a composer with a symphony. Rather, this is a relationship based on freedom between God and a, so to speak, free-standing creation, responsible for what it is by its use of possibility, while these possibilities always include openness to the effective presence of God.

This account of creation, therefore, is an elaborate answer to the question 'Why is anything at all possible?', which includes the questions 'Why has it been possible so to mistreat the planet and its inhabitants?', and 'Why is it still possible to do something to put matters right?'.

2. *Gelassenheit*: letting possibility be

Most doctrines of creation seek to show the connection between God and 'what is', but possibility is 'what can be', and the creation of that requires a different kind of metaphor from all designing or fabricating types of 'making'. Much more useful as a first move is John Macquarrie's description of creation as a 'letting-be which is prior to any is-ness'.

This letting-be is the creativity of Being,
and the dependence of the beings is their creatureliness.[2]

'Letting-be' is a suggestive phrase for God allowing to come into being a creation which is to be itself with its own character, however dependent it remains on having been let be. It retains the performative ring of the Hebrew $y^e h\hat{\imath}$ $\hat{o}r$, that is, 'Let there be light', *Fiat lux*. But what is brought into being in this account is possibility.

A model for the letting-be of possibilities may again be found within the existentialist fold, in Heidegger's account of what it is to let language be. He objected to all thought of language (and all language of thought) which was dominated by the desire to classify, for that in his view turned language into a given quantity of manageable stock available for human use, or indeed manipulation. That would give the appearance of control, but in fact such control would be inherently limited, more like a computer scanning its programme than the more open character of human creativity playing with possibilities.

Instead, Heidegger argued that language should be released, let be, for that alone would open out its own and its users' possibilities. I cannot pursue the subject of language here, but what Heidegger writes of the process may be transferred wholesale to a doctrine of creation:

> Anything that gives us room and enables us to do something gives us a possibility, that is, it gives what enables us. 'Possibility', thus understood, as what enables us, means something else than mere opportunity.[3]

I take Heidegger to mean here that possibility is not merely a chance to be seized by someone or something making the most of it. Instead, an emphasis on possibility redescribes any situation in the wider terms of openness, freedom and exploration; not being hemmed in finally by present circumstances or classifications.

Following Heidegger's thought one may say that what God let be in creation was not a succession of actualities which could form a manageable stock for human classifying and manipulation – not something so under human control – but was rather possibility, or, more exactly, the possibility of possibilities; that which makes any and every individual possibility possible. A perspective on the capacities but also the finitude of humans, however complex, intelligent, moral or spiritual they may be, is given by their existence among possibilities over which they never have total control, and which they can never exhaust.

Heidegger's concept was *Gelassenheit*, releasement, letting, which is certainly not passivity, but is an action only in so far as it becomes possible for things to be different afterwards. As John Llewellyn comments on the original text:

the *lassen* is neither quite as intrusively forward as actively to get, nor quite as reserved as passively to let.[4]

It is a valuable way to understand God in creation, for it is more creative and supportive than mere permission, but not determining in the way that causation is normally understood. It therefore expresses freedom without loss of power on the part of the one releasing, and a consequent freedom to experiment and explore for those let be.

As a description of God's bringing about creation this may appear to reduce divine action to even less than the deists' version, for they at least believed that God put together the design of the world. But their God showed only mechanical expertise, and when creation was complete (deists flourished before any doctrine of evolution) had nothing more to do, for the determinism of mechanism took over. But in this case letting be is not unconcerned transcendent dismissal (it is letting *be*, not letting *go*), but rather the enabling of what is other than God to have room to explore the possibilities of finite being and acting. Neither the bringing about of creation nor its result can be conceived of in mechanical terms, since particular possibilities and responses are not all predictable.

Such letting-be is again different from deism in that it is not a momentary initiative which starts everything off and is then withdrawn. Any individual possibility is transient, so to ensure the continuation of the possibility of possibilities and the enabling that this gives, the attitude of letting-be has to continue. *Gelassenheit*, therefore, is not so much a temporary (or temporal) action as the outcome of a disposition in a steady state, in theological terms providential as well as creative, which John Llewellyn describes as:

> composed steadfastness and patience [which] cannot be only prevenient, but must be sustained as long as the endurance is maintained.[5]

Thus there is built into the conception of letting-be the continuing patience and steadfastness of God, whereas in traditional doctrine the notion of providence had to be *added* as a distinct belief to the conception of God as any kind of initial maker of objects, or, indeed, of physical forces.

Thus far, therefore, this doctrine of creation concerns a God who let possibility be without designing how it should be fulfilled, for that would close down the enabling openness which *Gelassenheit* made possible. Moreover, possibilities continue as the constancy of the divine disposition towards creation continues. In that sense there is continuing creation, a continuing enabling of the possibility for things to happen and to come into being. But *what* happens and *what* comes into being is shaped by free exploration, experiment and choice at the time, though it is also always partly determined by prevailing conditions, which themselves came about through earlier possibilities being acted on.

Possibility is a necessary condition for there being anything to call creation at all, but within any particular situation a particular possibility is taken up by a creature within its current constraints and is thus contingently realized. At the same time, however, what comes into being (such as energy, antimatter, zebras, humans) comes as a response to possibility and thus as a response to the creator who let possibility be. So the very being of everything that is, has been, or will be, is both an acted-on possibility within entirely contingent conditions and simultaneously a response to divine enabling. Response is thus built into this model of God's creation, since some of the range of possibilities always have to be taken up for anything to be. In this way, even in the apparent abstractness of *Gelassenheit* a relationship of gift and response is implicit.

A gift, to be truly a gift, comes from the giver in freedom. There are no conditions on its donation or use. That God should let be what is other than divine shows the freedom of unbounded presence to let finite temporal presences come into being. Why God should allow this is a question more easily broached when love as well as freedom is in view in the next part of the book. On creation's side, what is given is the possibility to explore being and meaning with no divine blueprints attached to particular pathways; not even, I shall argue, the pathway to human evolution.

Evolution and history are not divinely designed. There is thus freedom to respond, a freedom which certainly has to be exercised in the midst of other finite freedoms with their own interests and values, but one which is in no way curtailed by God. To make use of particular possibilities is to respond in better or worse ways to the possibility of possibilities and thus to God; to have continuing possibilities is to have continuing occasions for response.

It would have been highly improbable that the whole concept of the world as a continuum of possibilities, some of which are always being chosen and acted on, thereby shaping actualities, could have arisen when Newton's physics furnished the principal answer to how things are. Such physics functions in absolute time and space within which, it was believed, given sufficient information, such as the position and momentum of an object, all is predictable, all is determined. There are no genuine, continuing possibilities, for the only properties of matter reckoned important were believed to behave with the reliability of a good machine.

Newton's physics remains useful in certain cases – quantity surveyors, for instance use it – but its range has been shown to be limited by the development of quantum physics. This is not the place to give a general account of the shift of understanding which accompanied the move from the macro to the micro world of sub-atomic physics.[6] The immediately important matter is that in particle physics it is impossible to deduce conclusively from a single measurement the behaviour of particles, or from any number of observations the behaviour of a single particle. Results are expressed instead in statistical averages which tend to 'remain stable if conditions remain stable'.[7] The conclusion often drawn from that is the one given by Davies and Gribbin: 'as a *statistical* theory quantum mechanics remains deterministic'.[8]

Even though the precision of machinery has gone, therefore, scientists ally their stable findings to the old certainties. Yet the emphasis on what is at least dependability has point. Otherwise the computer I am now using would not be reliable, although the behaviour of any individual electron in the machine cannot be predicted with certainty.

But in a late work, which can stand relatively independently from his other writings, the physicist and philosopher Karl Popper gives a different account of statistical stability in quantum physics, one which avoids the implications of determinism and links quantum physics to other sciences and indeed the whole of life in terms of possibilities. I have written of possibilities as if they were fairly inert ranges from which humans and other creatures could in some degree choose, and so does Popper at times. He has also, however, a vivid sense of multitudes of possibilities endeavouring to realize *themselves*, as if the *conation*, the creative striving to action, came from the possibilities. That is, perhaps, the only way to speak of possibilities for such insubstantial entities as particles, but writ large in the macro world it again gives a sense of the continual dance of possible becomings.

Possibilities, however, are differently weighted – in scientific terms from the *zero* of virtual impossibility to the *one* of virtual certainty. Popper avoids the appearance of determinism in the statistical stability of quantum physics by surmising that some possibilities are consistently weighted, and so are more like tendencies or propensities to realize themselves. Such propensities, he argues, are physical realities, 'as real as forces, or fields of forces', while forces themselves in physics may be described as propensities to accelerate (12). Reliability of effect, in that case, does not invalidate talk of possibilities. Rather it shows that possibilities can occur as high likelihoods.

Popper makes the important observation that possibilities are primarily inherent *in a situation* rather than in individual particles, or, for that matter, in objects or people. They also inhere in the way a situation may change. In a scientific experiment the situation is deliberately and totally put together, with unwanted conditions for the most part rigorously excluded. But that is still the locus of happenings where may be found 'the propensities to realize themselves which are inherent in all possibilities in various degrees' (19).

The difference in the scientific situation, therefore, is the degree of control over propensities in order to gain stable results, not simple determinism.

Popper can draw on other sciences to take his case further. In biochemistry, for example,

> it is widely appreciated that every new compound creates new possibilities for further new compounds to synthesize, possibilities which previously did not exist (17).

Thus a world seen in terms of possibilities is one which opens out more and more as, in the example from the fields of science, the fruitfulness of a theory or a research programme is explored. So possibilities used point forward to more and new possibilities, and thus the world, and the science of the world, continue.

Outside the strict controls of science, 'in our real, changing world, the situation and, with it, the possibilities and thus the propensities change all the time' (17). We, who are part of all our own situations, change them by our preference for one possibility over another, or by perceiving new possibilities.

> Our very understanding of the world changes the conditions of the changing world; and so do our wishes and our preferences, our motivations, our hopes, our dreams, our phantasies, our hypotheses, our theories (26).

Popper could have subdued this lyrical account somewhat by adding that our preferences, hopes or hypotheses have to co-exist with those of others and with inherited conditions, so that while change is potentially extraordinarily diverse in range, it is often in fact much more limited.

Nevertheless, in science and out of science, the world can be understood in terms of possibilities being discerned or chanced upon, chosen and acted upon, while these actions themselves close off some past and present possibilities but open up others. The history of evolution can certainly be told in these terms, as the continuing exploration of what was possible in the environment and the survival of those who could make use of the possibilities.

> It is especially obvious in the case of the evolution of life that the future was always open. It is obvious that in the evolution of life

there were almost infinite possibilities. But they were largely exclusive possibilities.[9]

By that Popper means that the choice/accident of one actualization, especially if it proved successful, could exclude and destroy other possibilities.

As a consequence, only comparatively few propensities could realize themselves. Still, the variety of those that have realized themselves is staggering. I believe that this was a process in which both *accidents* and *preferences*, preferences of the organisms for certain possibilities, were mixed: the organisms were in search of a better world (13).

It will be clear that Popper's descriptions embody a way of viewing the world which will change conceptions of causality and determinism.

3. The play of possibilities: exit the First Cause

Anyone who has watched snooker competitions on television has seen graphic instances of the paradigm case of Newtonian cause and effect. One ball is directed across the green baize to hit another with the further motion of both balls affected by the impact. The empiricist Hume may have warned that causation *as such* is not strictly visible: what is *seen* is the movement of ball A followed by the movement of ball B and the changed action of A. But he allowed the attribution of causation to imagination and the custom of seeing A and B in close conjunction. However, such subtlety could hardly have been maintained in the burgeoning success of science and technology where machinery was understood in terms of one part driving another. Indeed, Kant concluded that causation in that sense was simply a category of human understanding, brought to all experience of the phenomenal world to make sense of it.

Part of Newton's revolution was that action could happen over a distance – pull rather than push – like the gravitational attraction of the Moon affecting tides on Earth. But although that was scientifically important, it did not change the calculable before and after sense of cause and effect greatly. That sense had been in place since Plato and Aristotle, for whom rest (not Newtonian motion) was the natural state of any object. For them it was movement that had to be explained, and that occurred only when something was acted on. So causation, one way or another, has been understood in terms of what Popper calls 'push'.

R. F. Holland speculates on the origin of the sense of causation in small, every-day, taken-for-granted actions and effects, so that problems arise when the scope of causation is broadened and *events* are said to cause further events. The simplicity and completeness of the experience is then lost.

> Our knowledge of causes and their effects is rooted in cases where there is immediacy, where there is not enough of a gap in space or time for the insertion of a wedge that says 'unless'; it is rooted in our familiarity with the more obvious causal properties of common substances like water, wood, wrought-iron and stone, and in our use of simple but effective instruments like the crowbars and hammers with which we prise things apart or knock them together; it is rooted in the causal transactions whose unsusceptibility to upset is always and everywhere taken completely for granted by us and relied upon without question as part of the permanent background of our lives.[10]

In such cases causes may indeed be said to occur; it is the extrapolation to cover all cases of before and after which is dubious.

The description thus far has been of causation among actualities, as if actualities were all, and all causation could be determined from the past acting on the present, and was predictable on the same grounds into the future. Bringing possibilities into consideration, however, changes the picture. In that case, as Popper remarks, the classical cause 'is just a special case of propensity: the case of propensity equal to one' (22). But the point is that in the diverse and changing world beyond Holland's basic instances there are always many possibilities, and it cannot always be predicted which will be equal to one tomorrow. In a similar vein the French philosopher

Bergson inveighed against conceiving possibility as a kind of ideal (i.e. non-material) pre-existence of the actual which was less real but discernible, and caught up in the process of cause and effect.[11]

What both Bergson and Popper wish to argue from their very different standpoints is that the future is always to some extent open. In Popper's terms:

> there are many possibilities trying to realize themselves, but few of them have a very high propensity, given the existing conditions (22).

Tomorrow at noon some of these will have become zero, or very small; others may have increased. At the moment, in the existing conditions, the likelihood that I shall go to a certain conference is small: if tomorrow I hear from the Travel and Research Committee that I have a grant towards the cost the probability will increase almost to one; if I hear I have no grant the possibility will decline to zero.

> At noon, those propensities that realize themselves will be equal to one in the presence of the then existing conditions (22).

It is evident from my own small example why Popper always refers to existing conditions as the matrix out of which propensities arise. Our world is structured from the possibilities which have already been acted on. So new possibilities have to occur within (or overturn) the present structure. But such possibilities do occur, the world changes and there is no totally closed nexus of cause and effect. What Popper describes is neither the push of Aristotelian or Cartesian causality nor the pull and push of Newtonian action, but the jostling co-existence of many possibilities whose inter-relationship with existing conditions brings about what happens.

Even within the stringencies of a scientific experiment which, as Popper describes them, either exclude or reduce to zero all interference or disturbing propensities, notions of cause and effect have been loosened.

Cause became state of affairs which, *relative to an accepted theory*, was described by the initial conditions. *Effect* was that event or state of affairs which the theory, in the presence of the initial conditions, could predict (21, Popper's emphases).

The theory thus plays a critical interpretative role in the whole event and is itself one of the 'existing conditions' directing attention towards the *future* state of affairs. In the end Popper becomes quite scathing about the continued understanding of impact from the past being the only thing that moves the world:

Our inclination to think deterministically derives from our acts as movers, as pushers of bodies: from our Cartesianism. But today this is no longer science. It has become ideology (20).

To point up the openness of the world outside scientific experiment, Popper recalls the old story that Newton was led to his account of gravity by watching an apple fall. This is an important example in its reference to the 'real' world, because it can be argued that an insufficient sense of the ways possibilities interact in the natural world has led humanity into thoughtless and destructive behaviour. In Newtonian scientific terms of cause and effect, the apple falls because of gravity and its fall can be calculated. But:

Real apples are emphatically not Newtonian apples. They fall usually when the wind blows. And the whole process is initiated by a chemical process that weakens the stem, so that the often-repeated movement due to the wind, together with the Newtonian weight of the apple, leads to the snap of the stem – a process that we can analyse, but cannot calculate in detail, mainly because of the probabilistic character of the biochemical processes that prevents us from predicting what will happen in a unique situation (24)

In the same way there are no simple predictable answers to such complicated real-world matters as the contribution to global warming of, say, deforestation. Yet that is the world in which something has to be done about the environmental crisis. At the same time, however, the interaction of possibilities that makes action difficult also makes it *possible*.

There are two important consequences for theology of thinking of the play of possibilities leading to the future rather than causation as impact from the past. The first is the continuing openness of the world to present and future change, in spite of its structured state at any particular moment. I shall return to that later. The other consequence concerns the action of God which, both before and after Newton, has been understood in terms of a cause having effects. For Aquinas, God as First Cause moved creatures from potentiality to act. Working back from such axioms as 'all that is moved is moved by another', and denying the possibility of infinite regress, Aquinas arrived at the metaphysical principle of a God who stands to creatures as first cause stands to secondary causes. Although the principle was metaphysical, the effects were held to be known in human lives. In spite of the luminous theological sophistication with which this understanding was elaborated, therefore, it was still cognate with other forms of cause and effect. So Popper's blunt rendering may stand: 'the first mover is the first cause, and *all causation is push*' (24).

Aquinas argued on the basis of an analogy of being between God and creatures. But long after that had fallen out of belief, God was still held to be 'pushing', as for Newton the divine finger restored planets to their courses, and for Paley God's expertise showed in the marvellous contrivance of the human eye. In creation generally, and in human lives in particular, God's action was, and in many places still is, interpreted in terms of intervention and push, of being a classical 'cause' which produces classical 'effects'. But that belief has had sorry consequences in the last two centuries, with the rise of modern history and science, which could account for humanity and its world without reference to, or place for, divine intervention. As these 'effects' became increasingly difficult to identify, the connection with God as 'cause' disappeared.

The letting-be of possibilities is neither active nor passive; there is no clear effect and, arguably, there could have been no consequences. There is no inevitability, and so it is the opposite of push, or cause. It is rather, as Heidegger said, a continuous giving room to explore what is possible. Letting-be is the steady state of steadfastness and patience which allows a future rather than determining the present from the past, or diminishing creaturely possibility by intervention. Letting-be is not all that can be said of God, but only if creation is let be can divine love seek the other. Conversely, from creation's side, I shall describe letting-be as allowing God always to be found among the possibilities.

One last issue concerning the denial of God's action as classical causation concerns the popular modern version of the prime mover – God as the one who started the world with the Big Bang. It is tempting to see the Big Bang as the contemporary equivalent of Genesis 1.1: 'In the beginning . . . ' Here is a discrete event whose origin beyond the Planck time of 10^{-43} seconds (in vulgar fractions, 1 over 1 followed by 43 noughts of a second) cannot be discerned by any present theory. From that singularity came energy, the wherewithal for matter, and the expansion in all directions of the universe. It is easily understandable as an image of the moment of creation – the big push, even *putsch*.

But, quite apart from a preference for creation as opening on to the future rather than determined by the past, that will not do. For one thing, science does not stand still, and the Big Bang is no longer its final word. The universe may be a vacuum fluctuation from a virtual particle, or again it may be that the 'real-time' universe 'emerges' from a primordial 'imaginary-time' four dimensional sphere.[12] But one of the most evidently suggestive speculations would do away entirely with any point at which the 'hand of God' could be operative.

The Hartle Hawking conception of the boundary of the universe is of a sphere which would offer no edge in space and no beginning or end in time. If God is supposed to have set creation in motion, Hawking's question becomes relevant:

So long as the universe had a beginning we could suppose it had a creator. But if the universe is really completely self-contained, having no boundary or edge, it would have neither beginning nor end: it would simply be. What place then for a creator?[13]

Hawking's theories may not win total support, but whether they do or not, their existence is sufficient to prevent over-simple identification between a moment of creation (the last bastion of God's causative action) and the Big Bang. On the other hand, the universe as an edgeless sphere would be as much a response to possibility as any of the other four-dimensional constructs of physicists. God as the one who allows anything at all to be possible remains credible.

Yet if God is removed from all areas of vulnerable assertion in history or science, it could well be asked whether the existence of such a God, letting-be possibility, is compatible with any or every possible state of affairs in the world, so that in the end the affirmation of such a God makes no difference, is trivial and without content. There is substance in part of this objection. If creation is let be genuinely freely to go its own way, then the existence of God *must be* compatible with whatever way or ways creation took, or, more exactly, is interpreted as taking. No state of affairs would disprove God, because God has not caused any of them.

But the conclusion that this renders God null does not follow. Differences have been made. In the first place, possibility exists. That cannot demonstrate God's existence as some latter-day proof, however startling it is to think of the possibility of possibilities. But when there is belief in God, the gift of possibility says a great deal about what kind of God this is. Further, I shall be arguing in a later section that this creaturely freedom which has made things what they are is an opening on to relationships of love between God and creation: the existence of these relationships makes a difference. It is possible in these ways to affirm divine character and action without interpreting God as an efficient cause.

This way of looking at things frees God as well as creation. It is one thing to acknowledge that theology, written by time-bound humans, has to take place within a context of what is currently thinkable, and quite another to tie God down to particular actions and events as currently understood, even the Big Bang. Yet, if divine action is causation and therefore push, that is all one may do, in quest of moments of God's action and impact. But the changes which have characterized the Western world since the Renaissance, and which have accelerated with each succeeding century, have meant that each identification of God with a particular action has had to be disavowed and rethought. Alternatively, God is inserted in whatever gaps there are in current knowledge.

Certainly human Christian understanding of God will change from age to age, but the history of reversal in regard to specific attributed actions in the human and natural worlds, which are now otherwise explained, looks more like a history of retreat from concreteness to abstract affirmation. It has resulted in anxiety and insecurity among believers, and a fair amount of scorn among scientists. Against that whole way of thought, the divine letting-be of possibility on the one hand, and creaturely use of it for better or worse on the other, does not tie God down to specific causal action, but does maintain divine involvement and creaturely response throughout.

4. Possibilities in a determinable world

In Genesis 1 the process of creation involves distinguishing, setting boundaries and assigning positions.[14]

What is thus visible in Genesis, and has been an important part of doctrines of creation ever since, is a sense of the positive security of divine creation over against the negative dissolution of chaos. Genesis 1 is priestly theological pronouncement, but even when a more poetic wonder at creation is being expressed in the Psalms, the same orderliness in diversity is extolled.

The high mountains are for the wild goats;
the rocks are a refuge for the coneys (Ps.104.18).

Quotations of similar wonder at God the producer of order in creation could be adduced from most of Christian history. Perhaps it is worthwhile to include one from Calvin, since this aspect of his theology is so little known. He celebrates

> the greatness of the Artificer who stationed, arranged and fitted together the starry host of heaven in such wonderful order that nothing more beautiful in appearance can be imagined; who so set and fixed some in their stations that they cannot move; who granted to others a freer course; who so adjusted the motion of all that days and nights, months, years and seasons of the year are measured off.[15]

But the introduction of the letting-be of creation to make its own temporary and haphazardly upset orders overturns this entire tradition. God is not a cause, therefore not a cause of order, therefore not a guarantee of any inherent orderliness in the world. There must always have been problems with this affirmation, for instance in times of drought or flood, although these were theologically explained as punishment for sin. I shall return to the questions raised by natural evil in a later section.

Yet one of humanity's greatest achievements, the theoretical and practical advance of science, is said to have begun out of the belief that God's world would be ordered and hence intelligible. To this day, with or without belief in God, belief in the intelligibility of the world has to underpin scientific practice. Perhaps, then, there is more order than the ecological crisis would lead one to believe, and the crisis is simply a series of lapses from that order? The whole issue of science and the order or intelligibility of the world has to be examined.

There exists, especially within the scientific community, a 'principle of sufficient reason' which holds that satisfactory explanations may be found for why everything is as it is. Understandably, it is this principle which underlies scientific investigations, for these would be pointless without the presumption that explanations will be forthcoming in whatever area is researched. Following Milton Munitz, however, two aspects of this principle may be distinguished.[16] There is first the *methodological* principle of sufficient reason which is fundamental to the scientific enterprise. In order to go about its day to day work, the scientific community must act in the expectation of reducing the matter under investigation to intelligibility, and will not be satisfied until an explanation is found. As a method, the principle of sufficient reason is not necessarily at odds with a world seen to include possibilities as well as actualities, and to have a relatively open future. The reasons methodically discovered may be seen in Popper's terms of propensities which have become one and were acted on. Thus an explanation could be given in terms of 'reasons' as 'realized possibilities'.

But secondly, Munitz describes a *metaphysical* principle of sufficient reason, which, he says, holds that there *must be* such reasons, such intelligibility, whether they can be found or not. That view is metaphysical because it decrees that the world (or the universe) is, in its very being, scientifically intelligible. The assertion of such total objective intelligibility goes well beyond anything that could be established by science itself in its individual branches, or collectively. Like all metaphysical principles, it is the reflection of a belief, in this case concerning the objective scientific or mathematical reasonableness of the universe and the world within it.

The perception that this may be believed, but cannot be demonstrated scientifically, is in one way simply another instance of the boundaries of human thought. It is analogous to the difficulties any philosophical system has in defining 'truth' from within the system. (Moreover, I shall shortly have recourse to the similar findings of the mathematician Gödel that axioms cannot be shown to be consistent from within the system.) A philosophical example is that the statement 'Truth is correspondence to fact' has itself no discoverable fact with which to correspond, and therefore, from within the system, cannot be shown to be true. What happens *de facto* in philosophy is that what is valued and trusted is taken as truth, and the system is then built around that.

In the same way, in science a particular kind of rational intelligibility in both the study and the subjects studied is valued and taken as truth to give a metaphysical underpinning to the scientific enterprise, which, for many scientists, could not be conducted without some kind of faith. That particular faith, however, impinges upon my description of God creating possibility whenever the description of a particular intelligibility assumes some kind of final closure of possibility and an inherent determinism. That may happen in some scientific appeal to laws, to which I shall return, but it shows supremely in the current desire for a 'theory of everything'.

Thus a belief in the scientific reasonableness of 'everything' (in practice, everything relevant) is a driving force to the total explanation of everything. Currently this is most evident in cosmology using 'superstring' theory

> as a serious attempt to amalgamate all the fundamental forces and particles of physics, as well as the structure of space and time, into a single, all-embracing mathematical scheme.[17]

That would be a Grand Unified Theory (GUT), or a Theology of Everything (TOE). But as Willem Drees points out:

> Science is in *practice* . . . at odds with complete necessity. In trying to explain everything, science always traces properties or events or rules back to other events, boundary conditions or laws. Certain rules are used in that process of explanation, laws of physics and logical and mathematical rules.[18]

Thus explanations for everything become more 'fundamental' and aim to conclude with certain simple principles. But, asks Drees, why these principles? Any chosen principles will remain contingent. Even if the hope were to be fulfilled that the principles agreed with all observations, they could not be held to rule out the possibility (always possibilities!) of a *different* set of principles leading to a *different* universe. Further, the principles themselves cannot show the *necessity*, as opposed to the contingency, of the existence of anything corresponding to them, since they were derived from within the chain of explanation.

Paul Davies makes similar points against the possibility of a unique superunified theory – and if a theory explains finally why everything is the way it is, it would have to be unique. All contingency would be eliminated. In the first place, he argues, 'theoretical physicists frequently discuss mathematically consistent "toy universes"'.[19] In that case something more than a demonstration of mathematical consistency would be required for uniqueness, since a toy universe could have that. There is, moreover, the problem of Gödel's theorem for all theories which would be complete and coherent. That is, it is impossible to prove that axioms are consistent from *within* the system of axioms. On the other hand, 'if consistency can be shown, then the system of axioms will not be complete, in the sense that there would exist true mathematical statements that could not be proved to be true within that system'.[20] This is the same kind of point as Drees was making: necessity cannot be proved from within any system of thought or mathematics.

The determinism implicit in a 'theory of everything' is therefore systematically impossible, and what Drees calls 'conceptual bound-edness' is as much in evidence in science as elsewhere. He quotes Isham:

> Like most things in life, theoretical physics does not yield something for nothing, and what you get out is what you put in,

and concludes 'that theories are bounded by the concepts used and the assumptions made'.[21]

Without the theories there is no intelligibility – which is not the same as saying that there is no universe to interpret, but only concepts. The existence of the universe or the world around us is not denied, but what is affirmed is that humans cannot work without assumptions, principles and concepts, which are both the foundation and the limiting factors of scientific, technological, philosophical and, for that matter, theological, success.

Earlier I suggested that a world in which possibilities continually arise is one which can never yield to humanity a manageable stock over which they have total control. Change, novelty and difference keep occurring in such a world; new perceptions arise; new interpretations are made. From different points of view that seems to be a good thing. In the first place, humanity's history gives one no confidence in its capacity to handle such power as total explanations would yield. Then, again, it would be intellectually stultifying to have arrived, to have the equations which demonstrated all that had to be known: we would become servants of the equations, just as an earlier generation feared becoming servants of the machine.

Nevertheless, there is apparent physical order in the world and the universe, just as there are social, moral, intellectual species and other orders. In that case indeterminism is also an unsatisfactory thesis, unless it means simply that determinism goes too far. But if indeterminism is equally metaphysically held, with a belief that everything is always open and fluid, it goes against both our experience of order with its constraints (to which I shall return) and the way in which sense can be made of physical order by means of theories.

It is often thought that determinism and indeterminism exhaust the possibilities for describing the way the world is. But there is a third possibility which allows for human conceptual boundedness and for change, as well as the order found at any particular moment. That is, that the world is, physically, socially and so forth, *determinable*, capable of being temporarily determined and redetermined as circumstances change. That is the evident deduction from the varieties of ways in which the world has been perceived to be ordered – in science, in its brief span, as much as in any other field. Reordering is visible even in cosmology. It appears that the more knowledge a theory about the universe *incorporates*, the shorter it *survives*. The mythical view lasted for millennia; Newton's for some centuries; the Big Bang based on Einstein's general relativity for decades.

Thus experience over time is of the ordering and reordering of a world, and a universe which responds to human intelligence and activity. The world is both presently shaped and yet reshapeable where a difference can be made. I shall return to what an orderable world implies for the status of knowledge, but first I wish to argue that only an orderable, determinable world will allow the exercise of creaturely, and perhaps especially human, freedom.

Freedom is usually thought of only in terms of an agent being sufficiently unconstrained to be able to think, choose and act. But more is required than that, for interpretation, choice and action in an unyielding world would have no effect. As I argued in an earlier book:

> Freedom requires also a set of circumstances plastic enough to interpretation and decision to be acted upon.[22]

Freedom, of course, can be curtailed by previous decisions and their effects. Circumstances are not always plastic: but if they are not, that is because prior freedom among the available possibilities has closed them for the moment at least. They would remain closed if the world did not continue to be determinable, to be shaped and reshaped into new orderings. A determinable world which can be, and indeed must be ordered for life to continue, but whose orderings can be changed, is a necessary condition for creaturely freedom. It is also the kind of world one would expect when possibilities as well as actualities are recognized as being part of reality.

A world that is determinable puts considerable responsibility on to its reflective and powerful human inhabitants for how best it may be shaped. The ecological crisis would not have arisen unless human beings had been free to shape conceptions of the natural world according to their convenience and profit. But the world remains determinable, and things can be changed.

5. Laws of nature and the determinable world

One matter which is often held to transcend this openness to change and consequent relativity (i.e. a relative relativism, where knowledge is more than opinion, but less than timeless truth) is the laws of nature, and in particular the laws of physics. John Polkinghorne argues in this vein, and looks to the laws as a reliable framework given to the world by God, within which contingency functions:

> I believe that the regularities of natural law are pale reflections of the One who is their Ordainer.[23]

But if the world is entirely determinable, and creation is entirely free, not even the laws of physics may have this fixed role.

Within the Newtonian paradigm, which was itself deterministic, a law of nature was the apogee of determination, and evidence of God's handiwork. As Alexander Pope wrote:

Nature and Nature's laws lay all in night,
God said, 'Let Newton be', and all was light.

It was then believed that laws were derived directly from experiment, were universally applicable, and always enabled correct predictions and, where necessary, retrodictions.

The contemporary physicist Paul Davies in *The Mind of God* may be less mechanistic about the information which gives rise to a law, but he is as certain as any Newtonian about a law's objective standing.

The existence of regularities in nature is an objective mathematical fact.[24]

Laws are then constructions reflecting these reliable properties.

Without this assumption that the regularities are real, science is reduced to a meaningless charade.

But then he goes far beyond writing of necessary methodological assumptions. Laws, he claims, are something like God. They are *universal*, that is, they work for everyone everywhere; they are *absolute*, for they depend on nothing; since they derive from mathematical structures they are *eternal*; nothing escapes them, so they are *omnipotent*. The very terminology of 'law' first derived from the belief that God, who had the qualities Davies describes, decreed them for the running of the universe. However, for Davies himself the regularities expressed in the laws, however God-like they are, are just there.

A more studied consideration of the laws of nature comes from the philosophical realist Rom Harré. He looks at various kinds of laws and finds them to be 'descriptions of abstractions or idealizations from a somewhat messy reality'.[25] Laws come from experiment, with the experimenter written out in the abstraction, and, on the theoretical side 'from some deep assumptions about the nature of the phenomena in question' (35). These assumptions are focussed in a theory 'in the heart of which is a model or analogy which represents the generative mechanisms that produce the phenomena the law describes' (44).

For Harré, laws are less God-like because, although they are constitutive, what they constitute is (only) what they can be made to encompass, which is not necessarily all that is. Nor does the law represent the only way things may be constituted. Here, for instance, is Harré's comment on Newton's first law of motion, which goes to the very foundation of his physics:

> Of course every body must continue in its state of rest or inertial motion. Anything that does not is thereby struck from the role of materialship. *Newton's law defines or specifies a universe.* It is regulative and constitutive, part of the way we specify our world (110f.).

Laws thus *define* rather than *describe* a world.

Laws, Harré holds, may be general or hedged about with restraints. They are something more than records of regularities or dispositions (like the disposition of a radio-active atom to decay), but their dependence on theories makes them less than absolute. While nothing *in its province* is normally excluded by a law, there is a good deal of 'somewhat messy reality' it abstracts from. In the end, and as part of its defining role, 'a law of nature tells us what kind of things, events or properties (all else being equal) go along with what' (114). But the necessity of a natural law comes from its connection with a theory, and hence from the basic assumptions which are embodied in the theory.

Thus, as Paul Davies initially allowed, there are assumptions, the absolute *sine qua non* of all thinking. Assumptions may lead to fruitful interaction with the world, and an inspired use of mathematics, but because there are always other possible assumptions, there is no timeless objectivity about them. There is also a sense of *déjà vu* in reading confident assertions from contemporary physicists after reading the equally confident pronouncements of the Newtonian era. It is always possible that new assumptions and other changes may take place, as little foreseeable now as Einstein was to the eighteenth century. The way things alter is caught in J. C. Squire's riposte to Pope's couplet:

It could not last. The Devil, shouting 'Ho
Let Einstein be!' restored the status quo.

Laws depend on theories, and theories themselves have been held up as the possible area of God's objective work. Polkinghorne writes:

I will define a theory as a candidate for the verisimilitudinous description of physical reality throughout a prescribed domain.[26]

He allows that models may be various, but finds them to be no more than heuristic devices without any ontological pretensions. Theories he clearly regards as something else entirely. Polkinghorne is clear about the openness of the world to change; finds chaos theory (of which more anon) fascinating; is aware of the necessity of a point of view; but still places his trust that science gives true information on the real world in the role of theories, held with 'critical realism', so that natural theology is possible with the laws of nature given by God.

I am not a scientist, but I have some experience of philosophical questions. Because science is in the end *human* knowledge, the process of knowing will not be *toto caelo* different from that process in other human endeavours. It is from that viewpoint that I find Polkinghorne's descriptions of critical realism difficult. I will begin there before moving on to his application of the philosophical stance to theories.

Critical realism may be said to have begun with Kant. He believed that on the one hand animals 'knew' by sense perception alone, and on the other hand God, who has no distance from the objects of perception, knew them as they really were. Between these two was humanity, at some distance from what was to be known, and therefore, like the animals, dependent on sense perception. But, unlike animals, humans had understanding, and could bring the results of perception into concepts, by which they could comprehend the world. However, the effects of distance remain, and therefore a point of view is inescapable. Humans, in that case, comprehend the phenomena, the way things appear, rather than the noumena, 'things in themselves' which God alone knows.

Kant's version of the context of human knowledge largely put an end to any lingering analogies between human knowing and divine knowing. Moreover, leaving aside the dubious positing of noumena, this version made human knowing more problematical than the empiricist version of sensation and reflection (found in Locke and Hume) would initially suggest. For empiricists the distance between the knower and the known enabled a purchase on understanding, and their way of knowing is consonant with what scientists have in the past understood themselves to be about. However, for Kant distance produced the inescapable limitations of perspective as well as the benefits of a vantage point. That distance and limitation does not necessarily mean that human understanding will never penetrate to true information on whatever is 'out there'. Rather it implies that *there is no way of knowing whether it does or not.*

Much modern philosophy of science, in which the *context* in which science is done has assumed a much greater importance, may have Wittgenstein as a recent forebear, but the views of Kant that we know things as they appear lie in the background. That contextual shift need not mean that scientific explanations are reduced to being 'nothing but' products of their intellectual and social context, as if there were nothing outside to explain. Rather, it is that attention has moved from the description of scientific explanation in terms of deduction and law (Popper, Hempel), to one which includes the activity of the scientific community in framing theories.[27]

Thus, to the irreducible human limitation Kant perceived, which is not removed by the use of mathematics if the material universe is still what has to be explained, the contextualist shift has added smaller, time-bound limitations of assumptions, models, matrices of thought and practice within which science operates and which direct its values and vision. From that perspective on perspectival working the degree of human input into theories and laws is more apparent.

Equally, it is from this background that Polkinghorne's definition of 'critical realism' appears inadequate. He writes:

I take a critically realist view of our scientific exploration of the world. Such a position implies the possibility of gaining verisimilitudinous knowledge, which is reliable without claiming to be exhaustive.[28]

Again, he describes himself as:

a self-confessed critical realist who believes that, through the verisimilitude achieved by well-winnowed theories, we have learned many things of the greatest significance about the world in which we live (49).

Polkinghorne's language is certainly for the most part cautious. The second quotation speaks of 'belief' and 'significance', and the first of knowledge which is 'reliable', none of which claims too much. But the word which keeps appearing is 'verisimilitude' or its adjective. Again this shows a measure of caution because it is not 'truth' that is being claimed, only something very like it. Yet here the old philosophical questions return. 'Verisimilitude' may have been used because truth is a difficult claim. But, if one does not know truth, how would one know that the likeness to truth had been obtained?

Polkinghorne's answer lies in the undoubtedly rigorous process that generally accepted physical theories go through so that there will be a final match between what is expected in the theory and what is discovered in the world. This is basically a correspondence theory of truth or verisimilitude, and has the same difficulties as all correspondence theories in being able to show that correspondence has taken place. Theories may be held to be confirmed by discoveries, as the Big Bang theory was confirmed by the discovery in 1992 of ripples of wispy clouds in the galaxy, which are an indication of the later 'clumpiness' of matter. That is certainly how science works, and from its success it elicits a good deal of trust. But it has had its failures, and the point remains that truth or its likeness cannot be demonstrated from beyond the matrix in which it is said to occur.

The importance of the matrix is again illustrated by the way Polkinghorne describes the rational inquiry which is to underwrite the sifting of theories.

> It is the satisfaction of very general criteria, such as comprehensiveness, simplicity and fertility in further development, which should be the distinguishing mark of a truly rational enquiry (7).

These, however, are by no means universal criteria. To someone who is not a scientist they do not have the same compelling force. For instance, the study of history is surely a rational inquiry into the past, but there simplicity is seen merely to fudge the complexity of human action, from which comprehensiveness cannot abstract, so that a historian's comprehensiveness is cumulative rather than general, while fertility in further development is much more individual and random than it is in a communal scientific research programme. None of that sense of complexity and contingency in events and interpretations makes the pursuit of history any less rational.

What emerges is that comprehensiveness, simplicity and fertility have different meanings and values in different intellectual areas. Even if science is privileged over history as giving an account of the basic constituents of the world, it still has private, not universal, values. Just as Rom Harré described a law as specifying a world, so science specifies here with its values how to go about finding a match between thought and the world. Like history, it is an interpretative process.

There is finally no area of human thought, in laws of nature or theories of physics, which escapes human limitation. Indeed it may be that very limitation which makes humans so successful in the empiricist mode. 'What works', as scientific theories so often do, may be relied upon until it proves untrustworthy, or something else turns up. My own argument does not escape the problems I have described. I am having to declare the limitation of human thought as if that affirmation itself escaped such limitation, and could be applied universally. But that problem is again simply part of the

general bind with *all* philosophical systems, or mathematical systems
of axioms, that their view of truth, verisimilitude or consistency
cannot be demonstrated from within the system.

Thus the *critical* aspect of critical realism acquires more force than
Polkinghorne gives it. Human thinking is done by humans within
their varied contexts. But there is no logical or necessary progression
from acknowledging human limitation in knowing to denying the
existence of the world or the value of human rationality within these
confines. In exactly the same way there is no logical or necessary
progression from human limitation in thinking about God to a denial
of God's existence. The sole unarguable conclusion is that human
thinking has its limits.

This line of argument has been developed against the notion that
laws or theories have an objective truth given by God, which runs
counter to the belief basic to this book that God let be, and did not
design any of it. In the discussion I did not pursue the theological
point that a very odd sense of God emerges, as the one who designed
the laws of physics with minute particularity, but then let the hurly-
burly and pain of creation take their course without further
precautions. Instead, part of my argument is that the very notion of
truth is relative, though not useless. Human truths come from
human exploration of such matter as the environment, or the past, or
the capacity to think. They are part of the use of possibility, which is
how the world goes, and thus they are a response to God the creator
of possibility. But they never cease to be human. It cannot be denied
that human reason has often been fruitful, and not only in science.
On the other hand the very existence of the ecological crisis is a
demonstration that 'fruitfulness' is often absent. A little humility
concerning reason on the part of our species, both in and out of
theology, would not be inappropriate.

Disorder: exit the Cosmic Designer

The emphasis on possibilities thus far is not intended to deny the
existence of order in the world, indeed of many orders which give
sufficient stability for lives to be lived, beliefs to be held, business to

be conducted and research to give results. There is nothing in experience to suggest the radical indeterminism of a world which cannot be trusted anywhere, ever, for regularities. My point is not that order is not experienced, but that, extrapolating from all the variety and change in the past and present, it appears that any particular perception or experience of order in knowledge, in society or personal life, is contingent, vulnerable to upset, and has at all times to co-exist with other orderings unless it becomes temporarily dominant.

An order may work successfully, be widely accepted and prove fruitful. It will then be trusted. Indeed we have to trust the world we know and live in, if we are to live without paranoia. But, across the world and through history, order after order has collapsed or changed. In ordinary life change is forcefully seen in the requirement of present capitalism for consumers to embrace continual novelty in order to keep the world in business. Again, warfare and drought may undo orders in the human and natural worlds, while the writing of this doctrine of creation was prompted by such environmental exigencies. The crisis came about in our changeable world, and something can be done about it only because everything in the world is still open to change.

New perceptions create new possibilities of ordering, as chaos theory has worked with open dynamical systems which could not be dealt with, and hence were ignored, by previous scientific orderings of importance. Any ordering thus does exclude what falls outside it as well as giving a temporary stability to what it covers. But the change from one order to another in almost any sphere is experienced as disorder.

Disorder, of course, may appear to be simply destructive, as when the Norsemen raided the British coast, burning and pillaging villages and monasteries. Order was swallowed up in disorder. The phrase 'the end of civilization as we know it' could well have been used, had it been invented. While real pity may be felt for the sufferers, in the long historical view a new order emerged, as the invaders built themselves settlements and farmed the land they had taken by force, contributing eventually to the racial mix of Britain.

Some time after writing that example of the Norsemen, however, with the emphases I had once learned at school, I discovered that 'revisionist' historians now insist that there was little brutality in the Norse invasions, and that, for the most part, it was empty land they took over. In its own way such revision is another example of chaos, in that the previous orderly reading of the past is upset, but results in a new ordering. Such disorder leading to new order, in experience, historical accounts of the past, or in any other field, is what chaos theory, in its scientific way, is about. I deliberately began with a historical example because chaos theory is in many ways akin to experience outside the scientific laboratory.

It began with investigation into unstable weather patterns, and has been occupied with open dynamical systems, unlike the closed mechanical systems science inherited from Newton. Such systems, just like the weather, intermittently fluctuate before new order appears. The sequence may be somewhat simply presented as beginning with present order; then there is disorder (chaos); a bifurcation of possibilities appears; one path is followed, leading to a new coherence – and so the process continues.

The lack of equilibrium in a system is the vehicle of change to a new order.

> The timeless, totally determined physical systems built by Newton and still affirmed as universal by Einstein, have proved to exist only rarely, as limiting conditions of equilibrium. Elsewhere there is unpredictable fluctuation.[29]

Giving prominence to elements of randomness and unpredictability in systems leads to a world-view of spontaneous activity in matter with change constantly possible – in other words, a world open to determination and redetermination. Such a world is open to the future, and bubbles with possibilities seeking to realize themselves, as Popper described. Its order comes from those realized possibilities which have not yet become intolerably disorderly.

This is certainly an unsettled, and possibly a psychologically unsettling, version of the world. Within Newtonian dynamics one could always know where one was, in the most final way. But the price of that knowledge was the ignoring of anything that was not a closed system, while the knower was distanced from the inert objects of knowledge. Within the world-view of chaos, on the other hand, small possibilities may have large effects (the ubiquitous butterfly flapping its wings in one place and causing a storm in another), while instability is a continual possibility. The concern is with relations, interaction and change among parts of the system rather than with 'what there is' in any static sense of substance. Thus Prigogine and Stenger point to a move away from 'a concept of nature that would explain away the complex, and reduce it to the simplicity of some hidden world. Today interest is shifting from substance to relation, to communication, to time.'[30]

What is attractive in this scientific account, which makes the mapping of coastlines and the analysis of waterfalls possible, is that it echoes experience in the open systems of social and personal life. It is equally useful for describing the processes of evolution with its order and disorder, for often accounts may read like the ascent of order, with everything extraneous to that relegated to secondary importance. Again, the way an ecological system continues through fluctuations of populations is amenable to this understanding. Above all, from my point of view, it describes the open dynamical systems with which God as Creator is to be related.

The theological tradition has always attributed some form of deterministic design to God. Paul could point to the order of the world as indicating a Creator, and condemn those who could not understand that (Rom.1.19–25). Order in the natural world has been held to be so striking that it alone could lead the sensitive soul (in Romanticism) or the rational human to belief in the Creator. In the eighteenth century, when doctrine seemed obscure, and often downright contrary to reason, great comfort was taken from the orderly classification of species as indicating the order God had given nature.

There was, in fact, a kind of Protestant resacralization of nature. It is often noted that as Christianity spread, it forbade worship of local divinities in woods and rivers, and effectively desacralized the natural world. But in the seventeenth and eighteenth centuries, in the enthusiasm of naturalists like John Ray, a 'vegetative soul' was rediscovered at work throughout the universe.[31] Even those who would not go so far as that found a vivid avenue to God through the beauty and variety of nature.

> Ray stands in the long line of religious scientists who can see God at the end of their microscopes, who look to the book of nature for spiritual nourishment as much as to the Scriptures.[32]

Paley shares in the delight, but his intention is more apologetic and didactic. He is also more Newtonian, celebrating the mechanical genius of God designing creatures, as a demonstration of the benevolence of the Creator.

> Now, when the multitude of animals is considered, the number of parts in each, their figure and fitness, the faculties depending upon them, the variety of species, the complexity of structure, the success, in so many cases, and felicity of the result, we can never reflect, without the profoundest adoration, upon the character of that Being, from whom all these things have proceeded: we cannot help acknowledging what an exertion of benevolence creation was; of a benevolence how minute in its care, how vast in its comprehension![33]

Paley's formidable investigations in part prepared the way for Darwin's theory of evolution, and his conclusions concerning the deity were superseded by that theory. The Romantic view Wordsworth described as of 'a presence far more deeply interfused' in Nature (now capitalized and virtually personified) was equally undermined by the theory, as one can see from Tennyson's wrestling in *In Memoriam* with a Nature careless of both the individual and the type. Individual Christians struggled with the problems theology faced during the nineteenth century, but the tradition of God's designing order continued. Brunner gives classical expression to it in the 1950s.

> Sin is the human denial of the divine order of creation, but creation as a whole is not further affected by sin. Apart from the

evil in men's hearts, and in their actions, everything in the world is God's creation: the course of the stars, the changing seasons, the form and the life of plants and animals . . . the human body . . . human generations . . . all this is, as it is, and takes place in this way because, and as, God had appointed it, from the standpoint of his creation.[34]

One of the chief arguments against the notion of God as cosmic designer is the amount of evil in the world that cannot be accounted for by attributing it to human sin. Brunner raises this as a question, but never answers it.

For the more fully we ascribe – in our doctrine of creation – responsibility to God for that which is created, the more disturbing is our view of the actual reality. Can this world, so full of meaningless, cruel, suffering and death – be God's creation?[35]

The issue of natural evil is so profound, and so little attended to, that I shall come back to it in much greater detail in a later section.

The axiom of Christian faith that God is a God of order and not of disorder has meant in practice that disorder has been ignored, or explained away, or written off as sin. It has meant also that God is identified with whatever order, especially church order, prevails. The axiom shows, among other things, how important order is for human life, so important that its existence is equated with the doing of God. But that has left Christianity speechless in the face of much disorder, from ripples of change to total upset.

The emphasis on order has never reflected the dual experience of stability and change, the disequilibrium inherent in present order in open systems which is the basis of chaos theory. Even when the identification of God with designed order has not been part of a natural theology proof from design (and it is not in Brunner), it still shares some of the weaknesses of such an attempted proof. It is, in the first place, bound to be *selective*, concentrating on appearances of order and ignoring contrary instances. It is essentially *optimistic*, even when allowance has to be made for human sin, since order or design is thought of as a good thing. (Paley: 'It is a happy world after all.'[36])

Then, again, the tidy kind of God discovered in order is not one who would seem to be able to enjoy diversity and change, or share in the suffering brought about by disorder.

In contradistinction to all that, I have argued that God is not responsible for either order or disorder, but freely made it possible for creation to come into being, shaping and reshaping the world in the process. If freedom from divine structuring and design is part of the gift of possibility, the world that came into being has to be one that can be acted on. Freedom exists not only when action is sufficiently unconstrained, but also when there is a possibility of making a difference. So, if there is freedom in creation, the world must be such that differences may always be made.

Thus the only world in which possibilities are of any use is *determinable*, neither fixed in a determined order, nor incapable of being made orderly. A determined world has used up any possibilities it had, while indeterminism gives possibility no chance of fulfilment. A determinable world may be used to bring about necessary order and stability, but it remains determinable, so other orderings may bring competition and upset. A determinable world is undoubtedly strenuous.

The outcome of God's *Gelassenheit*, therefore, can only be a world in which the multiple finite freedoms which have been let be, explore their own possibilities and make their own orders. This is a creation whose components were able to cohere, and whose living creatures, in exploring their environment, could change it, and themselves in the process. But in God's steadfastness the possibility of possibilities will not be withdrawn, so the possibility of change and new order is always there. Some of the outcomes of God's free creation undoubtedly cause grief and suffering to other creatures. One cannot draw an optimistic picture of universal well-being or cooperation. I shall have to return to that in writing of a God of love as well as freedom. Yet without freedom and without possibility, for all their ambiguous effects, there would be nothing for love to move out to, and no possible relationships.

Part Two

Creation as Presence and Relationship

There is a sense in which the first part of this book has *disconnected* God from creation in the way that connection has traditionally been understood. That was the one-way connection of maker to made, designer to designed, thinker to thought, cause to effect, author of order to the orders of creation. The objections to that form of connectedness, most of them already rehearsed, are its vulnerability to scientific explanation and change; its inability to account for evil within a good God's creation; and, further on the theological side, the presupposition of a form of relatedness which does not allow creation its own being, nor one which gives God a real involvement in the opening out of what happens.

Instead, therefore, I have proposed divine *Gelassenheit*, letting-be, which is, in John Llewelyn's words given earlier, 'neither quite as intrusively forward as actively to get, nor quite as reserved as passively to let'. That is what brings about the possibility of creation. Possibility is *granted*, a verb with performative force which again is neither totally active nor passive, yet enables a new situation. But possibility is granted for creation's free use of it with no strings attached. Yet this *disconnection* of the traditional relation of maker to made, in any sense of made, occurs only in order to describe a different *connection* between God and creation in a two-way process in place from the beginning. *Gelassenheit* certainly remains the divine initiative without which nothing could have been. It is a gesture of divine freedom, but it shows also divine wisdom and love, in that creation is given room to develop, but is not abandoned: possibility is released, but creation is not relinquished. From the beginning the gift of possibility elicits the response of becoming and being.

As *Gelassenheit* encompasses the continuing possibility of possibility, it manifests the steadfastness and patience of God, but on its own it is too general for what has to be said of God's relationship with all creation in specific happenings, as possibilities are actually used. This second aspect of a theology of creation, therefore, is intended to display the connection of God moment by moment with the freely developing creatures in evolution and history, in terms of a loving presence in companionship with all that is, in all its variety and its individual better or worse. Both the letting-be and the loving presence attend the individual, the group and the cosmos. Part Two, then, begins with a description of the quality and nature of God's presence with *all* creation, not just the human part, and goes on to explore the paradigm of Jesus Christ, from which all such Christian understanding of God derives. Thereafter the implications of God's presence for the divine significance of all evolution and history will be addressed.

1. Pansyntheism

I regret introducing a new technical word, when theology is already replete with them, but 'pansyntheism' has the value of succinct expression, differentiating in one word the case I wish to propose, namely that God is *with* ('with', rather than 'above' or 'in') everything and everyone, in a way which preserves divine and creaturely freedom, but connects them in divine love seeking response.

Pansyntheism translates from the Greek as 'God with everything', so that, in the first place, there is nothing outside the divine presence – from quantum fluctuations to toads, to human politics, to the inflating universe, and whatever may be beyond. Everything, at all times, stands in the divine presence, which is as omnipresent, though not as contingent, as the air we breathe. God is present in, and hence part of, every situation for every creature, while that presence alters the final meaning and value of every situation.

But God, even on the most immanent reckoning, remains God,

not to be confused with finite creatures. There is infinitely more to God than a presence in creation. Nor are the creatures, so to speak, invaded or overwhelmed by this powerful presence. They have their limited freedom also. To maintain the distinction and the freedom, the preposition to use for the divine presence is 'with', rather than 'in'. In some religious expressions the difference made by 'with' is a minor semantic matter, yet overall that difference expresses something of the first importance in relation to the understanding of freedom. If God is 'in me' internally directing my thought and action, what has happened to my own freedom and responsibility? Or does God have to be held partly responsible for the ambiguities within my own best but human, limited action? Instead of that apparent duality, the sense of 'I, yet not I' in Paul's phrase concerning responsibility for an action is better explained as the effect of God-with-me, although the inevitably finite action will be mine, than as an internally-joined double action. Certainly it has been customary to say that God may be seen *in* Jesus Christ, or *in* a certain action, because these occasions disclose God. But that, I would argue, is a somewhat elliptical way of expressing the sense of concurrence (running together, or *with*) between God and the creature so that they are understood together.

The 'with' of pansyntheism thus guarantees divine and creaturely freedom, and places responsibility for their actions on human beings. But at the same time, divine involvement and relationship is never relinquished. This is not, on God's side, a conditional or accidental co-presence, but the working out of the divine steadfastness of *Gelassenheit* in the contingencies of time. Further, in line with the whole Christian tradition concerning God's love, this is not the presence of a spy or an accumulator of sins. Judgment on the intentional and unintentional failings of creatures in thought and action certainly occurs, for this is not a blindly devoted presence. But such judgment comes from a complete understanding of the circumstances, and exists only to send the fault to oblivion, so that the relationship may continue. God's is a loving presence, with which to share the joy of being and becoming, from which to find comfort and strength in sorrow, or stimulation to further and better action, and through which to find forgiveness for the misuse of possibilities and the encouragement to do better. All of that is implicit in 'God with everything', and its realization in the lives of creatures is always possible.

Another way of expressing this sense of pansyntheism is to borrow a second concept from Heidegger. I borrowed *Gelassenheit* as a sensitive rendering of letting-be, and now I wish to use his concept of *Mitsein*, with-being, to express this immersion of God in every creature's everyday happenings. Heidegger wished to avoid any abstract conception of being, and express being-in-the-world, which has to be being along with other existences. As Steiner expresses Heidegger's thought:

> To be human is to be immersed, implanted, rooted in the earth, in the quotidian matter and matter-of-factness of the world.[1]

'Being', for Heidegger, was, among other things, being alongside (*Sein bei*), being for one another (*Füreinandersein*), as well as *Mitsein*, being-with. All of them express the impossibility of human being without others, and the necessity for reciprocity among humans.

It is this sense of involvement and reciprocity in being that I wish to take from Heidegger and apply to God. There is, however, a major difference in such application. Humans have no option but to be immersed in the everyday, while it is God's free and loving *choice* to exercise *Mitsein*. Further, this being-with is not something God bestows only on humans, for it is in place with every creature in all the circumstances of its life-span – and beyond, as I shall suggest later. Moreover the concept implies reciprocity, and thus creatures are all, always being-with God.

Attention to this companioning God is therefore always one of the possibilities of creatures in their freedom. That is certainly the case for humans, and I shall argue that it may be possible for other creatures in their way as well. But because God observes the space implied by 'with' and denied by 'in', a space which allows freedom, there is also freedom not to attend, or not to believe in the existence of this presence. There is no way it can be demonstrated, and what one person may take to be divine effects may be differently accounted for by another. Ambiguity thus pervades a changing world of multiple finite freedom, even in relation to the one who let it be. But given this belief, the world and all that is in it acquires value, meaning and significance beyond the temporal because it is the subject of divine companioning.

I have already compared the omnipresence of God to the air we breathe, which in fact we take for granted and scarcely notice until it is absent or polluted. These harmful contingencies do not apply to God's steadfastness, so there is always a danger that God, even more than the air, will be taken for granted or scarcely noticed. That may be the risk God takes in giving creation freedom. But the theistic faiths show how this even, unchanging omnipresence of God may be made special and vivid for humans who need that assistance in recognizing and responding to it. They have focussed their attention on certain moments or people believed to be paradigmatic of what God is about, in order to interpret all other moments from that pattern. For Christianity the paradigm is Jesus Christ, and I shall come to describe that shortly.

But in the Christian theological tradition that paradigmatic moment has been understood as an *intervention* of God's, a descent of the divine Logos/Son from above. I shall later be arguing that such a view annihilates the freedom of Jesus of Nazareth, but for the moment I wish to remain with the limitations of the nation of a primarily *distant* transcendence. Such an understanding divorces God from creation, with the result that creation is the place where God is normally remote, if not absent. In that case, if God is going to connect with creation at all, it can only be by intervention from afar, breaking into the flow of created being by a divine irruption at certain particular places and moments. There are great difficulties in asserting such interventions against historical or scientific understanding, but at the moment these theological difficulties will be enough.

Instead of that partiality of temporal and spatial presence which must come as a superior power overwhelming the normal, pansyntheism describes a God always present everywhere, offering both reproach and encouragement, and above all saving, forgiving companionship. In a sense, pansyntheism takes what has tradition-ally been said of the constancy and fellowship of the Holy Spirit to make that the paradigm of the presence of God, rather than thinking of a distant God who then has to *send* the Holy Spirit in order to have a presence here. The quality of that presence becomes humanly clear for Christians supremely in Jesus Christ, when the action of God is made visible in Jesus' enactment of creation's possibilities in a full response to God. Here, in intensified dramatic form, Christians see what creation is about and what is possible in it. In the same way, derivatively, churches and worship services intensify communally the experience of God which is always possible in any individual life's contingencies.

Pansyntheism, therefore, with its emphasis on the omnipresence of God, in no way denies the infinite transcendence of God, nor the existence of the divine independently of all limited human thought or experience. But it does deny that God's dwelling, the place where God is to be found, is only or even primarily a distant heaven. Moltmann describes this distant view well:

> Heaven is the milieu nearest to God, his direct environment. The earth, together with the atmosphere and the seas, are the outskirts of his existence, his less immediate environment.[2]

But with pansyntheism there is no God observing from the centre to the outskirts that men and women are starving, homeless or oppressed, or that the planet is variously as risk. Rather, God is present with creation in all that suffering as well as in its joy. What God may be said to *do* in such situations will be explored in the next section.

If pansyntheism and *Mitsein* differ from the tradition of transcend-ence by asserting God's presence with creation, they differ also from what has often been said of immanence by their emphasis on God being 'with' rather than 'in' creation. Divine immanence has always been a minor theme in theology, if it has appeared at all. The major objection to giving it prominence has been the fear that it would lead to pantheism, in which God and creation are said to be equated. From the Hebrew Scriptures Christianity inherited a very clear distinction between the Creator and the creatures. The 'gods of the nations' around Israel might have been encountered in storms, or represented in statues of bulls, but Yahweh was above that. He might *use* these instruments ('you make the clouds your chariot', Ps.104.3), but was not to be *identified* with them.

Also in the Hebrew Scriptures may be found a fairly crude misunderstanding of pantheism as it appears in the making of images (e.g. Isa.44.9–20), as if worship of a god could always be dissolved without remainder into worship of the wood from which the idol was made. Thomas Berry asks, fairly enough:

> Why were the pagans seen as idolatrous? The divine always appears in some embodiment: no one ever worshipped matter as matter.[3]

Nevertheless, that mistrust of embodied deity persisted in Christianity – or at least in the Christianity of the official church. It aided the desacralizing of the natural world as the faith spread. Earlier belief had found the locus of immanent divinity in trees, wells, woods or mountains, and consequently treated them with respect. Christians denied the divine presence and where possible removed such landmarks, or else, as at Canterbury, built a church on a place already accounted immanently holy, but with that holiness now ascribed to the transcendent God.

Emptying nature of the divine presence was made easier for Christianity by its almost total concern for the human as opposed to the natural world. Nothing in that case was felt to be lost. The role of nature in the divine purpose was understood to be that of a storehouse created by God for human use. The residual divine relationship with nature in Christian understanding, therefore, became God's manipulation of it for human flourishing, just as humans themselves used it for their own good. Thus in the country one might pray for rain or fine weather to help the harvest, but have no conception of any immediate value to God of the wheat or the barley, or of the processes of farming themselves.

If pantheism is to be rejected, it is not because it comprehended a vivid sense of the transcendent within the natural world. It is more strange to think that a distant Creator God would take no further interest in creation for its own sake than to be impressed with a sense of 'the beyond in the midst'. Rather, the objection falls again on the use of 'in' for the presence of God, for such indwelling presence may quite swamp creatureliness. That, at least, could be the effect of ancient pantheism, and a description of modern non-Christian Goddess worship gives the flavour of what may happen to this opposite extreme to transcendence:

> In the Craft, we do not *believe* in the Goddess, we connect with Her; through the moon, the stars, the ocean, the earth, through trees, animals, through other human beings, through ourselves. She is here. She is within us. She is the full circle: earth, air, fire, water, and essence – body, mind, spirit, emotions, change.[4]

For all the vivid sense of immanent divinity expressed here, the independence of the creature's being and becoming, and the possibility granted of making responsible use of possibilities seem to be overtaken, so that creation becomes, so to speak, the manifestation of the Goddess, rather than something with its own being. But a God who let creation *be* is more concerned with how creation *is*, including its urban deprivation and overpopulation, than with powering like electricity only through its natural elements.

A modern, sophisticated version of God 'in' creation is the *panentheism* of process theology:

> Everything which is not itself divine is yet believed to be 'in' God, in the sense that he is regarded as the circumambient reality operative in and through, while also more than, all that is not himself: or conversely, all which is not God has its existence within his operation and nature.[5]

This is not the place for an extended consideration of process theology which pioneered the notion of God and the world in process *together*. It is also remarkable that many writers on theology with a scientific, particularly a biological, background, such as Charles Birch, Arthur Peacocke and Ian Barbour, have found in process thought a way to take account of science within theology.[6]

For all its benefits, however, it has some problems from the point of view I have adopted.

First there is the question of who acts, and who has responsibility on a panentheistic view. Norman Pittenger, in the quotation above, describes God as 'operative in and through' creation. But Charles Hartshorne, for one, is quite clear on the creature's capacity for action:

> It is not God alone who acts in the world, every individual acts. There is no single producer of the actual series of events; one producer, to be sure, is uniquely universal, unsurpassably influential. Nevertheless, what happens is in no case the product of his creative acts alone. Countless choices intersect to make a world, and how, concretely, they intersect is not chosen by anyone, nor could it be.[7]

But what is the role of the 'uniquely universal, unsurpassably influential' God? As described by Cobb and Griffin: 'One aspect of God is a primordial envisagement of the pure possibilities. They are envisaged with appetition that they be actualized in the world.'[8] This is not a God who let possibility be, and cared for how it was used; rather, this God in Platonic fashion 'envisaged' the perfect forms of possibilities and lures reality (by giving it an 'appetition') into bringing these specific possibilities about. That 'lure', as Pailin describes it, is 'to take just this rather than any other concrete form – although, of course, it is open for (the creature) to use its creative freedom to actualize one of the other possible states open to it'.[9] Thus God in process thought has a preferred option, an 'aim' for the creature, whose freedom in relation to that is to choose it, or perhaps fail, or reject it for something presumably inferior.

There are problems in that view, in relation to natural evil, problems which are not, perhaps, prominent for a biologist tracing the course of evolution. Given the degree of truth in 'nature red in tooth and claw', if these creaturely forms have fulfilled their aim, then the total aim envisaged by God must include the stress and death involved in food chains, the way in which some animals like cats play with their prey, and so forth. Nor can the clashes and suffering which occur be subsumed under some greater evolutionary good, like increasing intelligence or complexity, if God is equally present with each *individual* creature, and is not distantly observing the *process*.

Pailin refers to 'just this concrete form', but there is not, and never has been, any living version of a concrete form prior to humanity which could escape the possibility of being the prey to another concrete form, or of finding its competitors superior. Geach's comment has point:

> Another blind alley, in my opinion, is the idea that God willed to produce a varied fauna and flora in our world through evolution by natural selection: as if this global strategy somehow let God off responsibility for the pain individual sentient beings may incidentally have suffered in the course of evolution.[10]

It is important that this pain of the individual creature, whatever creature that be, should be taken seriously, and not played down as just the way things are in the natural world with the connotation that this is how God intended it, or that it has no divine or theological significance. The rough and tumble (to put it no higher) of the natural world has come about, not because it was part of the divinely designed aims, but because this is how multiple interacting freedom in the use of possibilities developed. God is present, but not responsible, when a cheetah brings down an antelope just as much as when a gunman shoots a human target. God's presence cannot be diluted, nor is it directed only towards human beings. Until Christian theology recognizes that the life of all creatures, including its suffering, is lived in the presence of God, to whom it has value, its attitude towards the natural world will remain negligent, and the ecological crisis, that culmination of human negligence, will not be truly addressed.

There is an overarching teleological thrust inherent in panentheism, with God *in* creatures luring them onwards and upwards. But the problem with such teleologies is that the process becomes more important than the individual, while the goal (complexity) defines the only relevant canon of value, so that everything else is judged by that, and falls into insignificance. I shall develop that argument later. But at the moment it can be said that if God is present with each individual, whose very existence is a response to possibility, then that is true of God with, say, a polyp from a coral reef, a form which has survived effectively in its simplicity for something over five hundred million years, although now it is under threat from the warming oceans. One cannot say that polyps have resisted a divine lure towards complexity; rather, they have continued to be adequate, 'fit' in their environment, and it is possible, too, that God enjoys companionship with this fitness down their brief, uncomplex generations.

But the increase in ocean temperature, a by-product of human excess lethal to corals, acquires its full Christian seriousness when God's prior, millennia-long enjoyment of the corals and other threatened marine creatures is understood. Men and women, even with Christian beliefs, have not understood this, because they have not valued all creation in its relationship with God. When human beings act in the natural world, they do not enter a *terra nullius* (no one's land), to give the phrase used originally of the colonization of Australia. Just as the Aborigines were seen as 'no one', that is, no one who mattered, so the creatures of the natural world have been seen as non-mattering, with nothing in their being apart from usefulness to humans to give them value. But if God accompanies *all* creation, there is no situation in either the human or the natural world without divine value, no situation in which human beings may act as if God were absent or uninvolved.

Panentheism, then, with its emphasis on the process of evolution, tends to disregard the life-chances of the individual. An even wider, Platonic view of creatures is developed from process emphases by Keith Ward in *Rational Theology and the Creativity of God*. For him,

> the amazing variety of organic life forms can be seen as realizations of archetypes [devised in the mind of God], ordering the parts to the maintenance of total organic systems, and urging the species on to further experimental realizations of them.[11]

This view allows Ward to celebrate the objectively-given beauty of the world, for its contemplation becomes 'the dim apprehension of the manifested forms and patterns of the divine mind and its values'. Then, with no overt sense of a problem, or indeed of outrage at the chequered history of evolution, Ward writes:

> The cosmic mind, it seems, is no great respecter of individuals, biologically speaking: but it strives incessantly to produce system, harmony and the existence of the largest number of compossible values.[12]

The individual in non-human nature is utterly lost in this panorama, and has no value at all in the divine overview of system and harmony. If such a thing were suggested of individual humans in the midst of social systems, there would be a religious outcry. But is it not presumptuous to believe that God cares for each individual human being, but not for each endangered lemur of Madagascar, being concerned only with how the *population* fits into some archetypal harmonious whole? That would be the level of concern of a population ecologist, but God, surely, is something more. With such a broad sweep the whole question of evil, natural or perpetrated by human beings, within the natural world is simply dismissed as irrelevant. For Ward, presumably, divine harmony includes the food chain, which is certainly an efficient enough structure, but what of the temperature changes in the history of evolution before humanity appeared, which brought about extinctions? Since species were wiped out then, one could ask whether the divine mind tires of its productions. And if it does, why should Christians be involved in trying to preserve some of them?

It is by taking infinity and omnipresence seriously that *all* creation may be celebrated as existing in God's presence, since there is nowhere that God is not – including the disappearing forests of Madagascar. It is one of the values of Moltmann's picture of God in creation that he also begins with the infinity of God. But then, Moltmann suggests, God *withdraws* from the space in which creation will take place. Thus, before positive creation begins, the space which comes into being and is set free by God's self-limitation is a literally God-forsaken space. The *nihil* in which God creates his creation is God-forsakenness, hell, absolute death; it is against the threat of this that he maintains his creation in life.[13]

Thus for Moltmann there is still a 'nothing' in which God creates. This is like the nothing of the Christian tradition (*creatio ex nihilo*) which was expressed in the Greek words *ouk on*, an absolute absence of anything external to God, in contradistinction to the gnostic *me on*, which posited a usable nothing from which something could be made. God's total creative power was held to be demonstrated by the total non-existence of the *ouk on*, and it is this Moltmann has redescribed. But, having begun with the *infinite* God, he could not have the *nihil* outside God. So his nothing is nothing because God has left it, abandoned it by withdrawing into the divine self before coming forth again positively to create.

This makes a very powerful picture of the contingency of the world, poised over non-being, and held in being only by God's creative act. But it does throw up some theological problems. I do not see that infinity may be said to 'withdraw'. Certainly all talk about infinity is in limping human speech about something unimaginable, which is qualitative rather than crudely spatial. But infinity with, so to speak, a hole in it, is something less than infinite. An absolute diminution of God is posited here, however temporary, and that is more than self-limitation.

Moltmann is certainly right in speaking of God's self-limitation. To allow a finitely free creation to come into being is a form of self-limitation for the unconditioned divine. But the limitation is not one of space. Creation does not require that absolute (Newtonian) container space for its existence. One relevant way of thinking of space in this case would be to apply to it what Bergson wrote of time, seeing it not as absolute, nor even as flow, but as retardation: "Time is what hinders everything from being given at once."[14] That would be the character of time however it was measured. In the same way space could be said to be what hinders everything from being given in the same spot. In that case creation is retardation in the midst of the immediacy of infinity, so that possiblity can arise and things can happen. In that scenario there is no need for God to withdraw, and creation is permeated, but not overwhelmed, by the divine presence.

In that case also there is no need for Moltmann's posited condition of God-forsakenness, hell and absolute death as a nothing to which the positive actions of divine creation are opposed. 'Hell on earth' and the death of creatures are certainly things that happen, but they are not to be accounted for by the surfacing of a primeval nothingness into creation. Rather they are part of what it is to be finite, together with the ambiguity of creaturely use of possibilities.

Divine self-limitation, then, is not a withdrawal of God, not even a withdrawal as a prelude to a return. It has more to do with how God relates to what is not-God. No creature could stand what Rahner has called 'the burning, unconditional immediacy of God', and therefore there has been a long theological tradition concerning God's self-'accommodation' to finite creation.[15] What that accommodation is in terms of relationship, and how that bears on what God 'does' in creation, are matters which require separate consideration.

2. Relationship: the activity of God

What does God *do* in the world? In the days of biblical theology, when 'the mighty acts' of God were the central conception, it was relatively straightforward to say what God *had done*, in terms of divine interventions to save and punish as they are described in Scripture. It was considerably less easy to say what explicit, unambiguous mighty acts God had done since the biblical accounts. It is certainly the case that most biblical writers thought of God as intervening from without, but then they faced no problems for their theological viewpoint from rival, credible accounts given by science and history.

The difficulty in applying notions of God's mighty acts became clear in liberation theology. Its theologians introduced the vision of God suffering along with those who were deprived of peace and justice, and used the Exodus motif for an expectation of divine liberation, for which they, and such groups as the base communities, began to work.[16] But the outcome of such theology thirty years on is not what its writers hoped. There has been, certainly, a great deal of local raising of consciousness, while concerned people all over the world came to know of the state of desperate poverty in countries of the South, and at least put questions to such institutions as the World Bank and the International Monetary Fund. There are effects, and the slow percolation of influence.

But the local situations have not for the most part changed. Wealth in many countries of the South is in the hands of a small elite, and the poor, for whom libration theology proclaimed God's option, remain poor. There has been no Exodus. Work continues, but there is no *work* of God in the old biblical sense. What is left is the vision of God's suffering with the dispossessed and marginalized of creation, a theme which has been taken up widely, and certainly expresses God's concern, but in terms of effective, causative action leaves God as helpless as the poor.

A theology of the helplessness of God, built round the helplessness of Jesus on the cross, may indeed have something relevant to say to most societies about the misuse of power, and that it is not necessarily a show of power but the suffering of love that saves in the Christian sense. But suffering, as such, does not imply an intervention, or even interaction, on God's part with the world. If that is all that is said, God has merely changed from a powerful onlooker to a suffering onlooker, and creation remains on its own.

Something of the same criticism has been made by Keith Ward of process theology, in that although it holds that God provides an initial aim for all creatures, and lures them on to fulfil that, there is nothing that could be called interaction in the process.[17] God, in that case, seems powerless, a 'cosmic sponge' in Ward's language, soaking up experiences, but not able to direct the course of creation. This complaint perhaps underplays the amount of activity process theology posits in God's luring of creatures. Moreover, Ward's own account is scarcely more attractive, in that the grand divine purposes have no connection with well-being and individual freedom of creatures. But it is the case that nothing like mutuality of relationship, with its necessary interaction, is posited in process thought.

So what does God do? As I have described it, this is a world granted possibility whose actuality is entirely the work of creatures using that possibility of possibility. The sweeping numbers of extinctions in the history of evolution, apart from anything else, argue against belief in a divine aim for creatures, or, at least, for an aim most failed to reach; and if there is divine direction, one would have to say that it went through some catastrophic rearrangements *en route*. Creation, therefore, seems to me to be entirely free from God's shaping or directing hand in its development. Yet I wish to propound pansyntheism, that God is with everything and everyone, and I am sensitive to the complaint that God often seems to do nothing but suffer or collect experiences – although I believe God does both these things, and they are not negligible.

Divine freedom is not separate from divine love, unlike the case with human creatures, who rarely achieve their conjunction. So divine action will reflect both freedom *and* love. Too much consideration of God's action has been concentrated on what divine *power* might do without any reference to love, as if that were a secondary characteristic of God's, brought to bear subsequently and separately on human creation. But if love is the fundamental character of God, it is relevant to ask, 'What does love do?' and to respond that it does not manage the other; it does not use the other for achieving its own aim, but in a simple, perhaps overused, term which requires unpacking, it establishes and maintains *relationship* with the other or others. God's action, I shall argue, is the only one consonant with the divine character of freedom and love, which is the forming and maintenance of relationship with all the creatures as they evolve and act.

Thus the question 'What does God do?' resolves itself into 'What is it to have a relationship?' in a manner worthy of a God of freedom and love. For the most part human relationship will have to be the model, as that is the form humans most easily recognize, but God is not simply a divine human, nor is all creation human, so human models will not exhaust the possibilities of relationship. It is important to emphasize that the forming of relationships is action, indeed moral action. But it may, perhaps, be a form of action associated with women more often than with men. The 'God who acts' of biblical theology was a God who, in a male way, entered a situation and imposed 'himself' on it, much like a sheriff in a Western film. There are, of course, women who impose themselves, and men who are sensitive to relationship; this is a general comment made to underline the perception of relation-formation and -maintenance as worthwhile moral actions. Jean Grimshaw suggests, with due caveats and tentativeness:

> It might, for example, be the case, not so much that women and men *reason differently* about moral issues but that their ethical priorities differ, as that what is regarded as an important principle by women (such as maintaining relationships) is commonly seen by men as a *failure* of principle.[18]

'Relation' and 'relationship' at their most general imply connection – what one person or thing has to do with another. In ordinary use any kind of connection may be implied, such as a blood relation, connections in an argument, or the relation of parts as they interact in a machine. Again 'relationship' has been commonly used in recent times for a special connection, usually other than marriage, which exists privately between two people. As I shall use the term, however, relationship is neither so private and exclusive as in the last example, nor so impersonal and wide-ranging as the general use, although it owes something to both in its emphasis on choice and interaction.

In a freely-chosen human relationship, what happens first, phenomenologically, is the *noticing* of the other or others, so that, at least for the moment, one's whole concern is not concentrated on the self. Relationship is precisely what takes one 'out of' oneself, away from self-absorption and self-love. Indeed, noticing, that initial awareness, is only the first glimmer, for nothing will follow if no *attention* succeeds the noticing.

Attention takes time for the recognition of the characteristics and qualities of the other, recognition of the otherness of the other, and his/her power of attraction to draw one's thoughts from their immediate concerns. It is important to see that the only power exercised in this best kind of relationship is the power of attraction, not of force. What happens next, as the relationship begins to take root, is the process of *caring* how that other is, and a *sharing* of life, thought and action.

Sallie McFague attributes to the attention involved in relationship a whole epistemology, a theory of knowledge:

> Attention epistemology is listening, paying attention to another, the other, in itself, for itself. It is the opposite of means-ends thinking, thinking of anything, everything, as useful, necessary, pleasurable *to oneself*, that is, assuming that everything that is *not* the self has only utilitarian value.[19]

This is a possible, desirable, though difficult and rare condition among humans. But it does begin to describe the relationship God has with creation, a relationship which seeks the reciprocity of such attention from men and women back to God.

Relationship is essentially connection, the fulfilment of the persuasion 'Only connect' in E. M. Forster's *Howard's End*. Yet in this brief account of its possible path I have described it only from one side. Relationship may, in fact, be one-sided, perceived only by the one who recognizes, indeed lives, the connection of which the other may be unaware. It is important to insist on this within theology, for many accounts of the reason for Christ's death are given in terms of the *re-establishing* of the connection with God, as if the relationship were otherwise terminally ruptured by human sin.

But that implies a God whose love is *conditional* (upon sinless response) and one who would tolerate the breaking off of connection with creation. I do not believe that that describes a God of loving freedom, and the belief would not have arisen if the doctrine of creation had not posited a distant God. For, as Moltmann rightly says:

> If the Creator is himself present in creation . . . , then his relationship to creation must rather be viewed as an intricate web of unilateral, reciprocal and many-sided relationships.[20]

It may be the case that most people most of the time are curved in on themselves (Luther's definition of sin) and are unaware of any relationship with God, but that does not show there *is* no relationship. It shows only that people are unaware of it. When it is discovered, it is discovered as *already* existing on God's side, not something that comes suddenly into being, and certainly not something brought about by human repentance.

To talk of a divine relationship with creation, then, is in the first place to say that God's attention is directed towards it, in all its being, becoming and interacting. Attention is not simple observation, but the appreciative – and suffering – consideration of what happens to the other, while any real relationship involves caring. It has long been acknowledged that God cares for men and women in this way, but unless that is held to be true of all creation, there will be no good theological reason for being concerned about, say, the threat to species' population or habitat, or about the conditions of domestic rearing of livestock. At the same time, recognition of God's care for non-human creation cannot edge out reflection on God's care for the poor and underprivileged, upon whose suffering so much wealth and comfort has been built. *All* God's creatures are subjects of God's care.

God's initiative may thus be described as occurring one-sidedly, but if that were all, this account would still be vulnerable to a criticism that there is no interaction of God with creation here or any influence on how creation goes. But such attentive openness of God to creation is the basis upon which any interaction becomes possible. The groundwork is laid, yet such interaction remains *possible* rather than *obligatory*, since no mutual relationship of any worth can be imposed from one side. That, rather than any powerlessness, or divine withdrawal, limits God's action and is the divine self-imposed condition.

Relationship certainly comes to full fruition when it is *mutual*, when the attention and care flow in both directions without reducing the individuality or freedom of either, but adding to each the value given by the other, the sharing of common interests, and the enlargement of experience that relationship brings. Relationship thus effects change by influence, not by 'mighty acts', and that influence is often gradual, depending as it does on the sensitivity of the one influenced. What creation offers God in the mutuality of relationship, which is not the same as equality in relationship, will be the subject of the third part of this book.

God thus 'acts', not by special effort or thought, nor by the causative 'push' of which Popper was so scornful, but simply by the effects of the divine being-with on creation in the possibilities of relationship. Freedom and love are both engaged in the divine steadfast, attentive, caring continuation of letting-be and companioning the creatures. From such a presence all kinds of possibilities arise: particularly, I shall argue, possibilities of relationship in creaturely freedom and love. Sara Maitland expresses vividly the involvement I have attributed to God:

> If the cosmos, matter itself, exists in love, rather than for some bureaucratic or edifying purpose, it can, indeed it must, be free to grow, develop, evolve, change, experiment – profligately, extravagantly, randomly. The first ping into being of the first hydrogen atom *ex nihilo*, unthinkable and violently radical though that was, cannot be enough for love – any more than looking at your newborn baby . . . : you desire the thing or person you love to display more and more of what they are in the process of becoming, to change and grow and respond.[21]

3. Concurrence: the paradigm of Jesus Christ

Deism was the belief that God once designed the world and then left it to run its course without any further divine involvement. Opposed to that view was the traditional belief in divine concourse (*concursus divinus*) which affirmed some form of co-working between God and creatures, with the result that God, although transcendent, remained involved in how the world went. The description of that concourse has varied in the history of theology, and has included God as the transcendental cause sustaining secondary causes, or as providing the dynamism which enabled something new to emerge in creation.

This belief may be reinterpreted again when God's action is no longer understood as the exercise of causative power, but rather as the establishing and maintenance of relationship. Divine concourse was always a way of describing divine and creaturely joint action, so in this case it becomes the kind of concurrence (literally a 'running alongside') which occurs in a relationship. When any relationship is truly mutual its members think and act *together*, although each remains distinct in who or what he/she is. Each in individual freedom and out of regard, or even love, for the other, renounces isolation of thought and action in order to journey with the other in agreed concurrence. In human experience, of course, this concurrence is regularly fraught with failures and difficulties, since true mutual agreement in which neither member dominates and over- rules the other is rarely easy. Nevertheless, it is the degree to which concurrence is achieved that makes even human relationships worthwhile and viable. And as concurrence affects what is *done*, its effects show in action beyond the intimacies of the relationship.

The Gospels depict Jesus as acting in just such concurrence out of his relationship with God. He has times of prayer apart, but in public he acts for God in forgiving sins, in healing and exorcizing. Just as his parables illuminate the kind of words and actions in which the Kingdom of God becomes visible, so Jesus in his words and actions made the love of God visible for those with eyes to see. Those 'with eyes to see' are those who will notice and attend, participating in those first stages of relationship which involve a readiness to look away from the self, or the way things are now.

Jesus himself 'noticed' a widow giving her tiny, costly contribution to the Temple treasury, a paradigm of awareness of what is going on. He noticed Zacchaeus up in a tree, and by attention established a relationship between them which was also a relationship with God. The concurrence issuing from the relationship showed in the tax- gatherer's next actions, when he set about putting right his past overcharging. Thus Jesus shows the working out of concurrence with God among the people and the historical contingencies of his time, and that action had further effects in the spreading of freedom and love.

The power exercised in relationship is that of attraction, of drawing the attention and concern of the other without extinguishing that other's freedom. That is visible in Jesus' life also. He was there among the people; his words and actions were there for any who would hear or see. But everyone, including those who had already found their way to God through the law, and including even his disciples, had freedom to leave. No one could be compelled into the relationship and actions Jesus called the Kingdom of God if they did not catch the vision, if they did not respond out of their own freedom with some trust and love, however faltering. This was the risk Jesus, like God, took in working only by attraction, not by coercion.

Jesus' own actions showed remarkable freedom, including a freedom in relation to the religious organization of his day. Certainly he attended the synagogue and was not dissenting in that sense, but where he saw faith he said, 'Your faith has made you whole', or 'Your sins are forgiven', with no suggestion that the keeping of the law was a necessary prerequisite. In so doing Jesus incarnated an accessibility of God which made no religious conditions in offering love freely.

Implicit in that freedom also was Jesus' freedom from all the other barriers society puts up to make such demarcations as the superior from the inferior, or the acceptable from the unacceptable. He went among the poor, he stayed with a tax-gatherer, he cured a Roman soldier's daughter, he dined with a wealthy Pharisee and encouraged Nicodemus, a 'leader of the Jews', into a rebirth of vision. There were women in the group who travelled with him, and he did not shrink, as many 'holy men' might shrink, from the touch of a prostitute washing his feet. His good news was for all people, of all kinds, and it was in their service that Jesus used his freedom, so that love of God and love of the neighbour coalesced.

There is no hedging about of the holy here, no keeping it safe from the profane. Nor is there a powerful action-at-a-distance from God. Instead, as Jesus says in Mark's Gospel, the Kingdom of God, that expression of salvation, has come near, is present in the midst. Therefore, as part of the concurrence of action arising out of relationship with God, Jesus is open and accessible to all. Yet it is important to affirm that this incarnating of relationship with God was not a divine endowment, so that Jesus would have had no choice in the matter, but a human response, as can be seen from the way Jesus *learned* from a Syro-Phoenician woman to extend his openness beyond 'the house of Israel' (Mark 7.26).

Out of his love-directed freedom Jesus chose to go to Jerusalem at Passover time, even though it must have been clear that such a place at such a time would be dangerous to the free-speaking, free-acting Jesus. Such action, leading finally to Jesus' death, is again an expression of his concurrence with God. As such, it shows that there are no lengths to which love will not go, and no suffering it will not endure in the process of the relationship. The cross of Christ does not bring about the healing of a disrupted divine-human relationship, because that relationship is always in place on God's part. Instead it shows the cost of maintaining relationship in the face of opposition. From that perspective the resurrection is not the happy ending to a sad story, but the demonstration that God was there through it all and that the darkness of the cross has not put out the light of love. To see this and be changed by it is to find salvation.

The concurrence of Jesus with God is for Christians *the* demonstration of 'what God does'. However, for this account Jesus' ordinary human being is equally essential – indeed a humanness by full contemporary standards, not just by those of the first or fifth centuries. The 'true humanity' of Jesus has been affirmed by the church, but in the past that has been diluted to humanity-in-general, with no sense of Jesus as an individual person. It was not, in fact, until the rise of historical consciousness in the eighteenth and nineteenth centuries that the modern sense of the individual arose. It was also feared that if the human seemed to do more, God would seem to do less, as if action could be thus subdivided. But concurrence is a notion which allows for the combination of both: God with Jesus; Jesus with God, while the human and divine protagonists remain themselves.

So Jesus, messiah and saviour, is also the paradigm of concurrence because out of his own ordinary human freedom he responded to the presence of God to the degree that this relationship defined his thinking and acting. Therefore, for many who attended to this man, to see and hear him was to see and hear what God was about. But Jesus' freedom is never lost. He agonized in the garden of Gethsemane over the dangerous implications of his actions, but adhered to his concurrence with God. Throughout his life he made visible and effective the already-existing care of God for the poor and the sick, while through his parables he provoked people into thinking what kind of action God desires. An immediacy and directness about Jesus is portrayed in the Gospel accounts of his stories and actions which conveys the immediacy and directness of God.

This has been a very brief survey of Jesus Christ, designed only to argue for visible concurrence actually occurring between God and a human being. I have written elsewhere on further christological matters.[22] But one of the conclusions from this account is that it has been shown to be possible for a human with no special divine aspect to his being so to respond to God that the divine-human relationship comes alive so that freedom and love flow from the connection and are enacted in the world. That enacts, in the senses both of demonstrating and bringing about what God 'does', and that possibility is always open, even for 'greater works' (John 14.12), although the response to the divine initiative may also be limited, fragile or intermittent.

Creation and salvation are not two different acts of God, with salvation a rescue operation mounted by God after creation went astray. In relation to creation God's being there in freedom and love is always and already saving, because God's being, and the possible effects of divine presence, cannot alter or be diminished. But they can be ignored. Making possible, the *Gelassenheit* of creation, is also to make freedom and love *possible*, while God's presence as *Mitsein* makes them *available*. Jesus Christ is the incarnation of God, and is saviour, because in his words and actions (his concurrence) that possibility and presence became visible and effective.

Moreover, in Jesus Christ Christians see the *purpose* of creation by the creating-saving God. God seeks responses of freedom and love from creation, and the enlargement of possibilities of freedom and love within creation, however finite and fallible in local conditions the response and the concurrence may be. Divine presence in the midst of possibility makes response to that presence *possible*, thereby offering a mutuality of relationship which is not exhausted by individual and private enjoyment, but issues in concurrence, sharing the desire for freedom and love in creation even among the ambiguities its earlier freedom has already brought about. What that means for following Christ or concurring with God in the present state of the world will occupy the third part of this book.

4. Teleology now!

The title of this section is an adaptation from Francis Ford Coppola's film *Apocalypse Now!*, which retold the story of Joseph Conrad's novel *Heart of Darkness* in the context of the enormities of the Vietnam War. The point of the title, as I understand it, was that one did not have to wait for the winding-up of the world to experience the horrors described in Revelation (the Apocalypse) before the arrival of the New Jerusalem. They were known already in the journey to the heart of darkness in the all-consuming nature of warfare and what it did to the country and to the people involved, both Americans and Vietnamese. In the same way I wish to argue that neither the purposes of God nor the judgment and apotheosis of creation have to wait for some end-time when the books will be balanced. Rather, they are continually happening now, from moment to moment, and from possibility to possibility. A distant teleology goes with belief in a distant God who will sort everything out at the end. But when God is believed to be present, then every moment becomes eschatological, an end in itself, so to speak. Geach offers some useful models for understanding the importance of the moment: 'We need only consider the arts of song and dance rather than architecture to see that the final state need not be the point of the whole activity.'[23]

To arrive at the present urgency of teleology, of what God desires for creation *now*, the theological constructions of the last three sections may be put together. From pansyntheism comes the basic affirmation that God is with all creation, always. That divine presence is seeking response, mutual relationship and concurrence which echoes Jesus Christ's in the enlargement of freedom and love in this world. Thus the possibility which God let be has enabled possibilities which, for humans at least, with their sense of morality, exist so that within whatever conditions the freedom of creation has brought about, actions of freedom and love are to some extent possible.

Wherever love is shown, or freedom enlarged, there is concurrence with God's purposes, whether or not the relationship with God has been recognized. But where such relationship is avowed, and where Jesus Christ is held to be the incarnation of freedom and love, a sensitivity to the presence of God and the consequences for action are greatly increased. A great deal more could be said on the private, spiritual aspect of relationship with God, but in connection with a doctrine of creation for an endangered world, the *consequences* of relationship for understanding and action are of primary concern. The renewed understanding interprets the world in terms of the presence or absence of freedom and love, and action concurs with God in bringing about positive possibilities for these qualities. Thus, since this doctrine of creation is not divorced from belief concerning salvation, both imply that creation/salvation is something to be worked out as well as received. Indeed one could question what kind of relationship people have with God, even if it is avowed verbally, if there are no consequences in action, no sign of God's influence working to enlarge conceptions of what is possible and may be acted on.

In a nutshell, then, possibilities happen at every moment because God lets possibility be. God is present in every possibility, relating to all involved, and seeking a free, loving response which in humans will be moved to actions of freedom and love within the existing conditions that shape future possibilities. Christian action in the world, whether concerned with human or non-human nature, is built upon this theological basis.

Such action happens *now*, within the ambiguities and difficulties of any situation, while in a world of multiple finite freedom it remains

possible that the best-intentioned acts may have their own ambiguities. Jesus himself was not exempt from that in the variety of
response to his message and actions. But whatever the difficulties,
the purpose of creation is fulfilled in moments where such
concurrence with God takes place, and does not have to await some
final summation. Teleology, therefore, like the Kingdom of God,
has its locus in the midst, where each thing has its own importance in
the conditions in which it takes place, rather than losing its present
character in a directedness towards the end of time. As far as
creation is concerned, the Kingdom of God is the synthesis of those
moments where freedom and love become actual, while the
achievement of these purposes of God for the world are always
among current possibilities.

Moreover, God is eternal, and wherever there has been concurrence with God, I believe that God's involvement in that moment
makes it eternal as well. The fulfilments of God's purposes are not
lost, but are, so to speak, harvested as the fruits of creation. To the
unconditioned and the infinite there is eternal joy when the
conditioned and the finite may so concur. On the other hand, divine
judgment is that, although relationship is always maintained with
every creature, where there is no concurrence, or where there is no
renunciation of consuming selfishness, there is nothing to harvest.
These moments come under judgment, and fall into eternal
oblivion.

This account is a version of what God may be said to derive from
creation itself. It produces goods which God could have in no other
way than from the independence of creation in ordinary human and
natural situations being used to respond to the divine freedom and
love with its own limited and finite creaturely versions. There are,
certainly, differences here between the range of possible response in
human beings and that in non-human creation which I shall tease
out later. These goods from creation become possible for God
through divine self-limitation, the renunciation of any use of power
other than the attraction of relationship. They become available
within creation through human renunciation of the power to
dominate or advance the self in favour of the power of attention to

the other, catching the vision of freedom and love, and acting to bring these about. All that modifies what has been said of God's power and purpose, and of creation's intrinsic importance, in older versions of the doctrine. Some of these are worth considering now to point up the difference in thinking the ecological crisis has made necessary.

As a measure of how this account of the purpose of creation has moved away from traditional versions, it is instructive to consider it in relation to Brunner's writing in 1949 (ET 1952). He writes:

> The Christian idea means: that the purpose of the world is in God; that in it God wills his glory; in it he wills to rule; in it he wills to bring man – through his self-manifestation – into fellowship with himself.[24]

In one sense it is certainly right that 'the purpose of creation is in God'. In spite of variations in content, it has always been Christian belief that creation would not have come into being without God, and is no divine frivolity, but has its reasons. Even those traditional accounts of creation which see it as an overflowing of divine love rather than an exercise of divine will find a purpose in such emanation.[25] But in Brunner's account, like most of those in the tradition, the purpose of the world lies in God *alone*, both in its conception and its execution. Creation becomes simply some kind of instrument, however recalcitrant its human portion may be.

'In it God wills his glory.' This too strikes a very traditional note, namely that creation exists for the glory of God, indeed was created to receive that glory and reflect it back. Again, in a sense, that cannot be denied. A creation which owes its being ultimately to God, and which values its existence, will thank God for that, giving glory to the one who let it be. Yet the notion that God looks for divine glory reflected in creation, rather than values in the hurly-burly of creation's own life, sounds very like the story of Narcissus charmed by his own reflection in a pool of water. Moreoever, apart from the implication that God is concerned only with God, that version once more gives no value to creation, either on its own account, or in its relation to God. Its existence is at best a mirror, and at worst a distorting mirror of sin.

A neo-orthodox emphasis appears in Brunner's 'in it he wills to rule'. This describes a sovereign God whose relation to creation is one of willed dominion. Brunner does also write, in warmer terms than Barth at that point, of divine love imparted to creation, to be received back by God. But the framework in which he sets that love is one of dominion, far from the kind of relationship I have described where power is used to draw people to God rather than rule them, and where the otherness of the other is respected. Even allowing for Brunner's attribution of love, this is a 'Father knows best' kind of relationship, in which the role of the subject or child is obedience to the Father's wishes.

Certainly this vertical structuring and emphasis on obedience has a place in any Christian thinking, since God is God, while the danger of pansyntheism, as with all other descriptions of immanence, is that God will be reduced to the conveniently comfortable. But once more this relationship of willed dominion *expects* nothing from creation, and *values* nothing in creation except obedience. It is utterly unlike the parental relationship which gives a child room to explore and develop into a responsible adult, and then rejoices when there is free concurrence rather than imposed obedience.

The divine will to rule has a further limitation in a world conscious of the ecological crisis brought about by the callousness of human domination to the point of exploitation. In Christian belief the relation between God and human beings regularly becomes the ideal of all relationships, and is reproduced in the churches. When Christianity has God's dominion as the essence of divine connection with the earth, such dominion was in the first place reproduced in the churches, and then secondly in relation to the natural world which was to be obedient to human command. So when dominion, with increasing technical competence, became exploitation, churches with this priority in describing God had no theological basis for criticizing similar human behaviour, and could at best deplore its excesses. But if a doctrine of creation includes the response of creation to God, and consequent activity within creation, as matters with their own value to God, then action to increase that value and decrease its abuse in mismanagement becomes a priority.

The sole emphasis on God in the quotation from Brunner is modified in his last point: 'in it he wills to bring man . . . into fellowship with himself'. Here Brunner, unlike Barth, allows that human beings are able to hear the divine Word revealed in Christ, may be changed by it and drawn into fellowship. But to modern ears at least, there is something incompatible between 'God wills to rule', and 'God wills fellowship'. Fellowship is a form of relationship involving some kind of sharing, even if one has more to give than another, and such sharing is not possible within a structure of command-obedience.

The warmth that surfaces from time to time in Brunner's account of creation sits oddly with the then current view of God acting only *de haut en bas*. Thus on the one hand Brunner writes confidently that:

> Apart from the evil in men's hearts, and in their actions, everything in the world is God's creation.[26]

On the other hand he is clear that God has given creation freedom for response, and in that way has limited the exercise of divine power. But he can also write:

> Yet, because he *limits himself*, he does not cease to be the Lord of all that happens.[27]

Brunner is content to leave this incoherent juxtaposition of creaturely freedom and divine Lordship as a mystery to be made clear at the end time. But 'Lordship', given Brunner's emphasis on the freedom of the creature, can mean only that God initiated the possibility of free response. However, if that is all, and the freedom is genuine, the meaning of 'Lordship' is stretched well beyond its core conditions of rule. To use the kind of paradoxical language favoured by the neo-orthodox, it is Lordship used to renounce Lordship, so that the divine purpose for the world is to be achieved without Lordship. But in that case one cannot revert on occasions to Lordship as rule. In a sense my account is an advance on what

Brunner says of freedom and fellowship, but it accepts that such values involve a rethinking of how God relates to creation.

Brunner's final divine purpose for creation allowed for human fellowship, but that intimacy was not extended to the rest of the natural world. In his writing on evolution, or even on the independence of creation, Brunner has nothing to say on any relationship between the non-human world and God. To point this out is not to blame Brunner for not seeing what has become an acute theological issue half a century later. But it does show, in one of the few European theologians who took evolution seriously, that the consuming and lively interest was focussed on the human creature alone. Any survey of serious theological writing on the doctrine of creation for most of the twentieth century will support the accusation made against Christianity that it is overwhelmingly anthropocentric. During that time, when damage to the natural world was steadily increasing, theologians showed no awareness of any value to God, or any part of the purposes of God in the natural world. There were, therefore, initially no theological resources to draw on to oppose thoughtless human practices.

Even with ecological awareness, however, there are immense human difficulties in expressing such purposes in relation to non-human creaturely response. This teleology has been concerned with *relationships* and instances of *freedom* and *love* which have clear relevance in a human context, but cannot without more ado be transposed into the context of the natural world. Language and imagination have come up against their human limits. Theology is accustomed to such limits in relation to the infinite and therefore ineffable God, who cannot be contained within the limits of finite human thought and socially constructed language. In order to say anything at all of human experience of God, recognized traditions of models and metaphors have developed, a few of which take natural objects as their foundation, as when the solidity, shelter and permanence of a rock in the desert conveys these qualities in God. More usually, however, the best known forms of *personal* models are used, since relationships couched in these terms convey most vividly to women and men their connection with God.

Theological models for God may change, but what endures is that they are drawn from the realm of the personal. God is known not to be a person, but in the individuality of relationship the personal sense is so strong that theological conceptions outside their more rarefied philosophical reaches tend to be almost entirely in personal terms. As an extension to that, the Creator's relationship to non-human creation has been expressed as if God were a human with all a human being's limited understanding of other species. God is said to look on the heart of humans, knowing them from within better than they know themselves. But there is no such tradition of God knowing from within what it is to be an eagle, a crocodile or a virus, and therefore knowing how to connect with these creatures.

In that case, human limitation has a double effect. It prevents human beings from thorough understanding of what it is to be a non-human creature, and it has held them back from thinking that even God has the understanding to connect with that creature on its own ground, not on a quasi-human ground. For the most part human beings may only observe from outside the *behaviour* of other creatures and analyse their *structure*, although they may sometimes guess at their feelings. But when human feelings are inappropriately attributed, that is named the pathetic fallacy, i.e. the misplaced belief that nature, for example, has moods as humans do. There has thus been in this scientific society a *caveat* against projecting human feelings on to nature, but none against projecting human limitations on to God in relation to nature.

In *The Once and Future King*, T. H. White describes the magician Merlin's training of the young Arthur before he became king. That training included turning him into a bird, an ant and a fish, so that he might know intimately other forms of life and society. The book is still, of course, a human description of the life of other creatures, but it enlarges the human imagination in the way required to think of God's relationship with all creation. God knows as an ant knows what life in an ant colony is – and without the immediate antipathy that Arthur felt, since he still thought as a human being. Such a perception of God's presence and involvement may change human attitudes towards non-human creation. Even with our limited understanding, it brings such matters as the present catastrophes into vivid relief. Again, for instance, God knows, as a fish or any other river creature knows, what it is like when poisonous effluent flows into its habitat. (Even those who find it hard to sympathize with distant species may sympathize with God!) I shall return to that in the final part of the book.

Ascribing this version of teleology to non-human creation involves affirming that the relationship is in place on God's side with the totality of understanding which God shows towards human beings. The second stage is to insist that just as God cares for *individual* human beings, so the divine presence companions each individual non-human creature, with the result that teleology is *now*, in the life of that creature, and not in the whole process or in the entire system. The individual organism in its individual conditions, no matter how limited these look from a human point of view, is the outcome of God's gift of freedom and the subject of God's love.

That should not be taken to imply that creation matters only as a series of isolated individuals, for every individual human being is part of some networks, and is occasionally capable of community. Every individual non-human being likewise is part of an ecological system. The interaction is an important part of what it is to be that individual-in-relationship. Yet at the core it is the individual in his/hers/its own being and doing which matters to God.

This emphasis on the importance to God of the individual is one of the ways in which theology diverges from the overview of biologists and even ecologists, for all their helpful models of relationships among creatures:

> Literally ecology is the study of the earth's 'households' including the plants, animals, microorganisms and people that live together as interdependent components.[28]

That is the way we live, and any consideration of *how* we are to live has to be by attention to such households. But in the last theological analysis it is not as components that people, animals, insects and so forth have their importance. Nor is that importance in some place in evolutionary history. Rather, the theological estimation is more like the ordinary perception of the non-specialist.

> We human beings tend to think as individuals, and so, quite naturally, when we think about biological situations, we identify with the fate of the individual. We think in terms of a particular great tit – the one which nests in our garden or a nearby hedgerow. But natural selection does not work like this: it operates on the variations between individuals in any population to give direction to the development of that population as a whole. It channels the population into better adaptation to its environment and tends to be rather harsh on the individuals.[29]

In their study of natural selection, therefore, biologists of all kinds have understandably followed the process and the changes, and as a matter of method have not dwelt on the individual case. Moreover, the scientific attitude has been held to exclude feelings, so however much individual biologists or ecologists may find their subject matter full of beautiful or tragic instances, that cannot enter into the study as such. Theologians are under no such constraints; neither is God.

That sense of the value of the individual now! frees theology from all over-arching divinely-directed teleologies, including any in which non-human creation is of importance only as far as it contributed to the arrival of *homo sapiens* with its intelligence. Further, increase of complexity, from 'lower' to 'higher' creatures, ceases to be the major expression of divine teleology in evolution, although the range of possibilities which complex creatures have remains important as a measure of their capacity for response, their responsibility.

Human beings who regard themselves as the end-product of an upwardly-organizing process tend to celebrate complexity because that is *our* special characteristic.

> For the processes of the world exhibit an intelligible continuity in which the potentialities of its constituents are unfolded in forms of an ever increasing complexity and organization.[30]

But if human beings celebrate their top position as complex and intelligent, a cheetah might as well celebrate its top position in speed, or an elephant in strength. Again, what is often left out of account in that celebration is the human capacity for complex harm. But if what God desires is freedom and love in the use of possibilities, the important matter is the quality of use, rather than the range of possibilities, and the well-being of the creature now, rather than its place in the processes of evolution.

Teleology is now because God is in relationship now with the natural and human worlds, understanding everything that goes on and caring for the individual creature in the midst of its relationships. God's presence brings about a continuous realized eschatology where now always has eternal significance, a matter I shall return to in the last chapter. Although human beings will still use human categories of value in describing this, as they must, in relating to God thought of as personal and caring, still human notions of God's capacity and desire to connect with every creature are enlarged. The way in which creatures may be said to respond, so that there is a form of mutuality in the relationship, will be part of the description of the world of creatures which grew out of the divine gift.

5. The anthropic principle

I have been arguing against teleologies which emphasize the 'end product' as that which has value to God. But in the last twenty years this goal-directed view has taken comfort from the widely discussed 'anthropic principle', advanced mainly by physicists and their popularizers. It therefore becomes necessary to return temporarily to the realm of physics and cosmology to address the issues raised by this approach. Even a biologist like Arthur Peacocke adopts it into his providential scheme, adding only rather greater reference to the evolutionary process, since it coheres with the emphasis he places on the 'personal'. Peacocke describes the thrust of the principle thus:

> The universe appears to be such that it has generated through its own processes, following their own inherent principles of unfold-

ing new forms, a part of the universe (us) that knows that it exists in such a universe, and moreover, knows that it knows.[31]

There is a weak form of the anthropic principle, which is unobjectionable, if not particularly illuminating, as a teased-out tautology: the universe which produced the world which produced humans must have had the conditions which would produce humans, or we would not be here to observe it all. The universe and world also, of course, has had the conditions to produce the triceratops, the pygmy shrew, and the crocodile, all of which in their own way 'observed' it, if not with the intelligence and measuring tools of humans. As a tautology, the principle in its weak form may be adapted for all creatures.

But the drive, within physics and beyond, has been to prescribe a *necessary* place for humans within the development of the universe on account of their intelligent understanding of it. Human beings in that case become the *purpose* of the whole development. There are two sides to this stronger argument. First there is the extremely fine tuning of the initial conditions which produced the universe. To give one instance among many:

> If the expansive energy (resulting from the Big Bang) and the force of gravity had differed from equality by more than one in 10^{60} at a time less than 10^{-43} seconds after the Big Bang . . . the universe either long ago would have collapsed again to a Big Crunch, or else there would have been such run-away inflation that gravity would not have been able to pull any matter together to form stars.[32]

No current theory predicts that gravitational force, or any of the forces, or the values of a number of constants, like the speed of light. Observation alone discovers them. Yet these values and relationships have to be exactly and minutely right for the emergence of the universe. It is all highly improbable and staggering to contemplate. At the moment there is no scientific answer to why these conditions obtained. The anthropic principle appears to take the place of such scientific explanation in holding that the arrival of human beings intelligent enough to discern and understand these conditions is sufficient reason for their existence.[33]

The principle has not found favour with all scientists for two reasons. First there is the inherent uninformative, if not exactly vicious, circularity. The long scientific quest has hardly been worth the trouble if all that it has led to is, in Ferguson's formulation:

We are here because the universe is as it is, and the universe is as it is because we couldn't be here if it wasn't, and clearly we are here.[34]

Again, the anthropic principle with its intelligent observership as the teleological aim of the universe short-circuits all further effort at understanding the forces and the constants. Not surprisingly Stephen Hawking responded with:

Was it all a lucky chance? That would seem a counsel of despair, a negation of all our hopes of understanding the underlying order of the universe.[35]

In fact, work proceeds on explaining what was previously known only by observation. Seven particle masses have been derived from the theory of the Higgs field of energy, and confirmation is hoped from experiments at the particle accelerator at CERN which should identify a Higgs boson.[36] This continuing work demonstrates that scientists do not feel required to give up theory and experiments because the anthropic principle holds that the existence of experimenters is reason enough for the universe.

Another form of dissatisfaction with the principle is voiced mainly by those who are not physicists, who are aware of great improbabilities in their own field, and wonder why the initial conditions of the universe should be elevated to prime importance as if later improbabilities were negligible. Thus Stephen Jay Gould, the paleontologist, writes:

The central fallacy of this newly touted but historically moth-eaten argument [a form appeared in Alfred Wallace's theory of evolution in the nineteenth century] lies in the nature of history itself. Any complex historical outcome – intelligent life on earth, for example – represents a summation of improbabilities and becomes, therefore, absurdly unlikely. But something has to happen, even if any particular thing must stun us by its improbability.[37]

Gould is concerned primarily with the improbabilities he finds professionally in the fossil record, but Mary Midgley lists some other unlikely developments and wonders if they are more improbable than the development of human intelligence:

By what standards could one weigh the improbability of our hypertrophied cerebral cortex against – say – the improbability of a giraffe's hypertrophied neck and legs, or a fiddler crab's single gigantic claw? What, again, about the improbability of giant pandas, taxonomic carnivores who are complete vegetarians and live only on a single species of bamboo? What about colonial jellyfish, behaving like a single complex organism but built from a whole crowd of separate, separately reproducing individuals?[38]

Finally there is our own improbability, but this is more than our species' intelligence, special though that is. The biologist Lewis Thomas rhapsodized over the wonders of a living cell, and each individual's improbabilty:

We are alive against the stupendous odds of genetics, infinitely outnumbered by all the alternates who might . . . be in our places . . . We violate probability by our [physical] nature . . . Add to this the biological improbability that makes each member of our own species unique . . . You'd think we'd never stop dancing.[39]

There is nothing wrong with wonder at the finest of tuning which began the whole process, but it is only the first in a long line of improbabilities which may equally evoke wonder. My own personal wonder is aroused by the first meeting of my parents on the steps of a library. The day had turned wet, and my father-to-be offered the shelter of his umbrella to my future mother. If the weather had remained fine that day I would not now exist. But, as Gould wrote, something had to happen, or, in the language of this doctrine of creation, divinely-given possibilities were acted upon, and the result, for all the mess and sorrow there has been, is also something worthy of wonder. As Thomas wrote: 'You'd think we'd never stop dancing.'

Equally there is nothing wrong with appreciating the intelligence of human beings, even though that ambiguous capacity may give rise to intelligent evil. But alongside that, appreciation should go the valuing of other specialisms in creation – the craftsmanship of the weaver bird or the survival capacity of the crocodile. When all of these are valued together, rather than considering humanity's intelligence on its own, the anthropocentricity of Western and Christian thought will be greatly alleviated – to our own and the planet's benefit.

But there is more to the anthropic principle than has been discussed thus far. As it appears in the writings of the physicist John Wheeler it depends on the action of *observation* in the particular sense this has acquired in particle physics.

> Beginning with the Big Bang, the universe expands and cools. After eons of dynamic development, it gives rise to observership. Acts of observer-participancy . . . in turn give tangible 'reality' to the universe, not only now, but back to the beginning.[40]

That is to say, reality is effectually conferred by observation, and in an important sense does not exist prior to that observation. In that case observation is absolutely necessary to the full existence of the universe from the beginning. This builds on Heisenberg's realization that the act (or instruments) of observation in quantum physics determined what was to be seen, since the position and momentum of a particle could not be measured simultaneously.[41] Moreover probability waves function in the macro-world with an equal need for an observer to determine which one collapses to produce 'reality'.

Whatever may be the case with quantum reality, and there is a good argument that the different uses of the word show that 'reality' is something valued as much as described, the problem with Wheeler's formulation given above is the way it applies information theory to 'all that is'. That theory emphasizes the message sent and the message received. Wheeler wished to replace the notion of the universe as a machine, which underlay Newtonian physics, with the interpretation of it as a gigantic information-processing system with the output as yet undetermined. He coined the slogan 'It from bit', which is to say that 'every *it* – every particle, every field of force, even spacetime itself – is ultimately manifested to us through *bits* of information'.[42]

Information theory prizes the clarity of the transmission process between sender and receiver, like a message down a telephone line. Anything that gets in the way of such clarity is called 'noise', and from the point of view of information theory it is an unwanted intrusion, like a crossed line. Wheeler's description given above of the formation of the cosmos, and the intelligent observer conferring reality on it all, blocks out a good deal of noise. Everything about humans except the capacity some have for advanced theoretical physics is irrelevant, as is the whole ambiguous history of evolution, condensed by Wheeler into 'aeons of dynamic development'.

But arguably what is noise to this version of information theory is precisely what makes this world and all its past and present inhabitants special, uniquely themselves. Too much is lost in Wheeler's parsimony. Once more this may be contrasted with the view of Stephen Jay Gould theorizing before he discusses with affectionate particularity the extinct fossils of the Burgess Shale in his appropriately named *Wonderful Life*. This early burst of multi-celled organisms, whose fragile frames have fortuitously been preserved in the shale, would be scarcely a pin-fall of noise to Wheeler, nor to any teleology which prized higher-order complexity, intelligence or personhood above everything else creation is capable of. Yet they are there, part of the history of life on Earth, and in theological terms, part of creation.

The point Gould wishes to make is the importance of contingency, 'and contingency is a thing unto itself, not the titration of determination by randomness'.[43] Here Gould takes issue with all who would give a smooth account of evolution because *after* the fact *any* course of happenings may be described as inevitable, if the noise is cut out and only the smooth progression is left. But the creatures of the Burgess Shale, who flourished and died out, show that the story is not so simple. To get a real sense of evolution, the 'arrived' position at the end has to be abandoned in order to appreciate the continuous play of possibility and contingency. That, in fact, is how students of human history proceed.

Gould's position gives him an acute sense of possibilities in the way I have described them earlier:

> The diversity of possible itineraries does demonstrate that eventual results cannot be predicted at the outset. Each step proceeds for cause, but no finale can be specified at the start, and none would ever occur a second time in the same way, because any pathway proceeds through thousands of improbable stages. Alter any early event, ever so slightly and without apparent importance at the time, and evolution cascades into a radically different channel.[44]

Some slight alteration in the way things came about, then, might have sent evolution 'cascading' into a channel which did not produce human beings to observe the initial conditions of the universe, or to handle the world so callously that it is now in many kinds of trouble. It may be disturbing to contemplate our own non-existence, but in a doctrine of creation it is a worthwhile exercise, in order fully to appreciate that humans are not the sole repository of divine value. *Our* loss would be total, but there would still be plenty in creation for *God* to companion. It is a repeated theme in this book that doctrines of creation have in their anthropocentricity been shaped towards human fulfilment, rather than imagining what God might enjoy or gain from the whole process.

Gould notes that science has been slow to admit 'the different explanatory world of history' into its own sphere of thought, and has even denigrated history 'by regarding any invocation of contingency as less elegant or less meaningful than explanations based directly on timeless "laws of nature"'.[45] The work of some scientists consulted for this book would bear that statement out. Contingency is an endlessly individual cluster and change of circumstances, and hence too messy for laws.

But theology, surely, is less concerned with Wheeler's etiolated circle of initial conditions leading to observers of these conditions than it is with the inelegant contingencies of all that has been and is now. Theology is up to its neck in the churning mud of contingent existence (an image which reminds me of the trenches and confused battle-lines of the First World War) because that is where God is believed to be present. And if that is where God is present, then no comfortable teleology which abstracts from that contingency will do. Certainly God is present with human beings in all aspects of their life, from their physics to their warmongering, but God was also present with the realized possibilities of the long-extinct creatures of the Burgess Shale. In that case teleologies are little and local, and always 'now', because the divine companioning of creation is always now, with things as they are at present. The purposes of God in freedom and love are finding fulfilment or resistance *now*, and that is what finally matters.

The picture involved in this doctrine of creation is not one of God setting up the initial conditions with the express design to produce complexity and human consciousness and intelligence, but rather one of God letting be whatever would and could emerge from that freedom, and enjoying *all* responses of *all* kinds as they have occurred from the beginning of time, with their various qualities, of which intelligence is only one. With that enlarged interpretation Christianity may avoid the charge of anthropocentrism correctly levelled at it by those whose consciousness has been raised by the ecological crisis. From that point of view the anthropic principle in most of its forms is an extreme case of human hubris whose adoption into theology would eliminate all sense of creaturely interrelationship, or of divine value in the non-human world.

Part Three

The Companioned World

In their book *Good Omens*, Terry Pratchett and Neil Gaiman describe with great humour and a fair amount of incidental theological insight a world which may (or may not) be on the brink of Armageddon and The End. It is seen at times through the eyes of an angel, the one who first barred Eden with a flaming sword, and a demon, the one who in the guise of a serpent first tempted Adam and Eve.[1] Over the millennia of stirring up good and evil these two have established a rapport, if not a friendship, and they agree on how interesting the world is, and how enjoyable from both their points of view. Angels and demons, according to tradition, have fixed, unchanging characters, while the human and natural world is fluid and changing. It is, the demon muses, the area of grace, whose inhabitants are capable of greater good than an angel and greater harm than a demon because neither the good nor the evil is a *necessary* choice, nor is it dictated by a set character. The Earth is a world of possibilities, surprises, delight and distress, in which the particular events of the story unfold.

What the authors of *Good Omens* have caught is the way that an 'extra-terrestrial' view gives perspective to what happens on Earth. Such views, as imagined by human beings, are bound to be partial and time-bound. There was a time, for instance, when change was distrusted and equated with decay. Then the fixed angelic character was thought to be admirable, rather than lacking in variety and interest. But even allowing for such human limitation in the thinkable, such a projected extra-terrestrial view is required also in a doctrine of creation in the endeavour to say what creation is like, what it is for, and how God is involved at every point. Expressing the doctrine is less a matter of extrapolating certain features of the world into pointers to deity than it is of making a theological picture in which everything from the HIV virus to the most saintly human finds its place. In the process scripture, tradition, imagination, current understandings and experience all play their part.

Much of this 'big picture' is now in place. God let possibility be, and out of it came, as response, all that has ever been, is now, or will be. In its character of response, whether that character is recognized or not, the being of everything in all its contingent finitude is valuable to God, who in freedom and love companions it all. Thus every moment, for every creature using its possibilities, is spent in the presence of God. That is true of battery farm animals, of the myriad localized species of the tropical rain-forests, of human political processes; and true of both the writing and the reading of this book. God is always present along with the range, great or small, of present possibilities. Beyond that presence God seeks, not a simple reflection of divine glory, which would leave creation with no value of its own, but a relationship of concurrence, with each creature after its kind, a relationship between divine freedom and love on the one hand, and on the other creaturely freedom and love to the extent that these are able to exist in the ambiguous finite conditions of life on Earth.

If that, however, is the extra-terrestrial view, like the expanded diastole of the heart's action, it has to be made credible by intra-terrestrial arguments so that it is an explanation that works in life and practice as well as giving metaphysical direction. So, as the heart contracts in the systole, down to earth discussion is required about genes, about non-human nature's own disasters, about the differences, material and theological, between humans and non-humans. Without such proximate weighing of arguments the metaphysical theological picture could be wishful thinking. Yet, as the heart's action continues, so does the movement between God and creation.

1. Genes, environment and possibilities

The world, as I have described it, came into being as a response to possibility and continues as possibilities are acted on in evolution and history. At the same time, however, what has gone before has shaped any particular context with its continuing possibilities, just as blue-green algae, at an early moment of evolution, helped to produce an oxygen-rich atmosphere. Evolving creatures after that had to be able to breathe oxygen. But the shaping of the world goes on. It is never totally determined, since possibilities continue. It is, as I have argued, better described as *determinable*, temporarily determined by previous choices among possibilities, but remaining malleable to whatever can make a difference.

This view presumes a continuing degree of freedom for all creatures, although not complete freedom for any. Arguments opposing this attribution of freedom in thought, for humans, and action, for all creation, come from neo-Darwinians like Richard Dawkins, and socio-biologists like Edward Wilson. For Dawkins 'we, and all other animals, are machines created by our genes'.[2] Again, Wilson writes:

> The individual organism is only the vehicle, part of an elaborate device to preserve [the genes] and spread them with the least possible biochemical perturbation.[3]

Genes in that case have totally determined a creature's capacities, exerting 'ultimate power' (Dawkins) over behaviour – hence the machine model invoked to explain each individual organism. The survival of the genes is the only operative value in this account, and so they are called 'selfish'.

There is no doubt that the givenness of genetic inheritance is a constraint upon possibilities. Even when the mapping of the human genome is completed, so that there is some freedom in removing or replacing genes, that still applies, thus far, only to humans, and like most freedom it will be ambiguous, for the power of disposing of or inserting genes is open to abuse as well as benefit. The constraint of inherited genes, however, even of those which bring about harm, is not simply loss of freedom. Rather it helps to give definition to an area of real, continuing possibilities. Freedom is not necessarily a lack of boundaries, but rather the capacity to work creatively within or against these boundaries. But that is a credible view only if creatures are more than machines for the survival of their genes.

Dawkins and Wilson have been criticized for their emphasis on the *egoism* of genetically-induced behaviour to the point of denying that altruism is a genuine, non-self-seeking possibility. They have to find a 'basic' or 'underlying' selfishness in even the most likely cases of altruism. Evolution in this view is driven by something like Hobbes' war of all against all in the natural state. Mary Midgley objects to this over-individualistic account without denying the reality of genetically-based behaviour. All that is really required in the first place, she argues, is that altruistic behaviour, such as that among kin, should not prevent future gene-spread. That familial altruistic behaviour spreads unselfish tendencies, such as helping those in danger.

> And if we are worried about the primacy this gives to kin, we should notice that this is a very loose limitation. Because these tendencies do *not* spring from calculation, but from inherited disposition, they cannot be regularly switched off when someone less closely related heaves in sight. They are not strictly proportioned to blood relationship, but respond to many other cues, such as familiarity, liking and the special needs of others. And in human beings, the complexities of culture can give them a much wider range of channels than is possible for other species.[4]

So far from selfishness being the 'true' inheritance of human animals, then, there remain possibilities for affection, help and altruism, even within the constraints of genetic inheritance.

But how far do these constraints go in determining natural and human behaviour? Dawkins and Wilson write as if genes were the only relevant cause of creaturely behaviour. But that excludes any input from the environment, including, for humans, the cultural environment in which religion lies. Moreoever, the use of 'cause' in their discussions is open to the kind of criticism I have already made in Part Two. When these criticisms have been teased out the fatalism implicit in the selfish gene arguments may finally be questioned.

According to Dawkins, genes in each individual in each species alone direct behaviour. For non-human species, however, a different scenario is described by Niles Eldredge in *The Miner's Canary*, where what is important is the *interaction* of evolutionary developments and ecological circumstances. Certainly Eldredge is discussing extinctions, particularly mass extinctions, when the environment has exercised particular power. Changes in habitat, often the result of climate changes among other things, have had a decisive effect. But he would wish to extend that analysis of interaction to how creatures behave generally, and even to background extinctions (the way in which species regularly and unspectacularly become extinct):

> We know of nothing *intrinsic to species* which would suggest they can in fact run out of evolutionary gas.[5]

Evolutionary biology considers the history of genes, mutations and species down a time-line. Ecology looks at the mix of population of different species in one locality at any time, and how they fit together in their interactive niches. The addition of ecology to evolutionary understanding yields, in the first place, the perception of such 'arrangements' with the environment as co-evolution which is particularly perceptible when two species depend exclusively on each other. Thus a butterfly may have evolved to feed from a single species of flower, while the flower in turn depends on the butterfly for pollination. This evolutionary development into symbiosis is the stuff of many television wild-life documentaries. More generally, however, 'the adaptations of organisms of any given species are constantly being affected, each generation, by changes in other species that are also parts of the local ecosystem'.[6] If that is the case, more is at work in change than genes, and that 'more' is variable, full of possibilities and constraints.

Further, the degree of heterogeneity in the environment, that is, the number of micro-environments it can provide, controls the number of ecological niches which may be filled. No evolutionary change will have a chance of being passed on unless there is a niche in the local environment for the creatures to fill. It takes *varieties* of plants, for instance, to provide food for *varieties* of herbivores, which are in turn the prey of *varieties* of predators.

> Complexity begets additional complexity, but rests, at base, on environmental heterogeneity – the bottom line . . . in determining how many niches in fact will actually be represented in a given ecosystem.[7]

So, to genes and other creatures in an ecosystem has to be added the physical environment itself as a factor in what can come about.

There is a sense in which Eldredge could be seen as simply doubling the determinism which removes creaturely freedom – adding to the determination of genes the determination of the environment. But the environment is itself a collection of variables in interaction open to change. It does not have the givenness and omnicompetence Dawkins ascribes to genes. It is an area in which action and reaction according to the organism's capacities is possible. With articulate and self-conscious human beings, whose environment is not only the natural world but also culture, the possibilities for choice in action and reaction are greatly increased.

This muddying of the pure evolutionary stream through consideration of ecological fitness is in line with the argument of Susan Oyama in *The Ontogeny of Information*. In brief, she comments on the repeated pattern of Western thought in which one agent (God, Newtonian mechanics or evolution) is thought to be the sole imposer of order on chaos; she denies the appropriateness of the concept of 'code' for genes, let alone the transition from code to information or instruction; she argues that nature, including human nature, derives from a developmental process in which interaction and reaction are of primary importance.

> Genes affect biological processes because they are reactive, and this reactivity is a prime characteristic of our world, at all levels of analysis, from the subatomic through the social to the astronomical.[8]

Genes in that view still have their importance, but they are neither selfish nor the machine-minders of Dawkins' description. Rather:

> What we are moving toward is a conception of a developmental system, not as the reading off of a preexisting code, but as a complex of interacting influences, some inside the organism's skin, some external to it, and including its ecological niche in all its spatial and temporal aspects, *many of which are typically passed on in reproduction* either because they are in some way tied to the organism's . . . activities or characteristics or because they are stable features of the general environment. It is in this ontogenetic crucible that form appears and is transformed . . . Since even species-typical 'programmed' form is not one but a near-infinite series in transition throughout the life-cycle, each whole and functional in its own way, to refer to the type or the typical is also to refer to this series and the constant change that generates it.[9]

The picture that emerges from this discussion of reactive genes and a process of development in which the environment plays an active part is one much more like the openness to possibility I have posited for creatures than a closed inevitability of genes running a machine. Indeed any particular set of genes and any particular environment are themselves the result of possibilities acted on; on the genes' side possibilities running from the distant past of replicators and the beginnings of DNA to the mating of any organism's parents. Similarly Eldredge catches the first moments for ecology:

> When complex life first got going there was opportunity galore. Nobody was ahead of these life forms. Life had to invent ecosystems.[10]

And in a sense life has been inventing them ever since, as species, climates and habitat conditions have changed. When all that invention is seen from the point of view of a doctrine of creation, it is as a response to the Creator who let it all be.

The notion of *cause* used by Dawkins coheres with his advancement of genes as a single omnicompetent explanation in the machine mode. In *The Blind Watchmaker* he gives a hypothetical example of causation at work. A mutation in a beaver's genes leads it to hold its head higher in the water, thus preserving more sticky mud on the logs with which it builds its dam. A better dam leads to a larger lake and greater safety for the beaver's lodge. More offspring will then be successfully reared and the mutant gene will spread through the population of beavers until it becomes the norm. For Dawkins, therefore, 'the beaver dam evolved [into a more secure state] by natural selection' with eleven links in 'the causal chain linking altered gene to improved survival'.

> Every one of these links, whether it is an effect of the chemistry inside a cell, a later effect on how brain cells wire themselves together, or an even later effect on behaviour, or a final effect on lake size, is correctly regarded as *caused* by a change in the DNA . . . It is all perfectly simple, and delightfully automatic and unpremeditated.[11]

Dawkins' chief targets in *The Blind Watchmaker* are those who would see a divine purpose being worked out in the course evolution takes. For reasons that will become clear in following sections, including the mass extinctions which occupy Eldredge, I do not wish to argue for any form of divine direction or design in the manner of Paley, author in 1802 of the self-explanatory *Natural Theology, or Evidences of the Existence and Attributes of The Deity Collected from the Appearances of Nature*. The arguments against any such practice, once the theory of evolution is taken seriously, seem as compelling as those against perceiving the hand of God in historical processes.[12] I have no difficulty with the part played by a change in DNA in Dawkins' example. My difficulties come from the neglect of environmental factors already referred to (his beaver appears to have no competitors and no disasters; one may wonder, also, what the increase in lake size did for other creatures who lived in the area. But presumably Dawkins' is a history only of the winners), and the problem of his use of cause and causal links.

The instance of the beaver is a very good example of Oyama's perception of a preference for a single agent imposing effects. That is, perhaps, not simply Western, but typical of certain kinds of science. Historians, on the other hand, long ago gave up any idea of a single person, even as influential as Napoleon, say, being this kind of sole originator of events and effects. Oyama's comment on the privileging of genes into prime causal role has point:

> Much is written about the genes initiating, engendering and originating, and the idea of diminutive chemical engines powering biological processes is appealing. In fact, of course, a gene initiates a sequence of events only if one chooses to begin analysis at that point; it occupies no privileged energetic position outside the flux of physical interactions that constitutes the natural (and the artificial) world.[13]

So genes are an arbitrary starting point; in Dawkins' example, apart from any other 'physical interaction', the lake and the logs were there before beavers with or without a mutant gene. But moreover, the notion that they 'cause', in the sense of giving the only efficient push to, events is less than a fair account of the complexity of how things happen. In this respect also, evolutionary biology, when taken with its ecological dimension as well, deals with a hurly-burly just as history does, and could learn from the practice of historians, who have been refining their concept of causation for decades.[14] If poverty and unemployment, for instance, are thought to be among the *causes* of the French Revolution while in England there was contemporary poverty and unemployment but no revolution, what force can the notion of 'cause' have? The local interplay of possibilities and actions is much more subtle than any excerpted series of causal links would suggest.

I have discussed earlier Karl Popper's sarcasm on conceiving of cause as push from the past. Mary Midgley has expressed this well:

> To mechanists, no explanation counted as intelligible unless it worked upon the familiar model of push–pull, like the parts of the cog-driven machines with which they were familiar.[15]

In its place Popper puts the understanding of a whole raft of possibilities and propensities which are seeking (if one may personalize them) to become one rather than zero. That understanding could be transferred to an account of the French Revolution in its contingent happening, or indeed to whether the beaver's mutant gene would become the norm. I have cited also R. F. Holland's argument that notions of causation emerge from small, commonsense, indubitable examples of physical contact or force, such as crushing, mixing or pushing. But when these actions are extrapolated to notions of causation between *events*, as they are in Dawkins' example, the clarity and necessity of the small instances fail. What is left is 'a wonderfully diaphanous relationship'.

Since events lack all such properties as hardness, springiness, liquidity, porosity, causticity and tensile strength, there is nothing they can do but stand in ideally regular, universal-law-fulfilling relationships.[16]

As John Bowker recognizes, it is precisely this notion of an ideally regular universal law that Dawkins relies on.

There is no mistaking the nomothetic ambition of his work, which sits securely and uncritically in the positivist, covering-law camp: genes have a tendency to produce gene-survival machines, provided countervailing factors do not intervene.[17]

Covering-law theory with its aim to draw up the process of arriving at objective truth has largely given way in the philosophy of science to what Philip Clayton has called 'the contextualist shift' with its concern for the human processes of doing science as well as the results achieved. The only continuing role for formal covering-law thinking Clayton can perceive is 'as a regulative principle or guideline in the midst of a practice that falls far short of this (or any) ideal'.[18] Yet Dawkins implies a law which is to apply always and under nearly all conditions.

It is undeniable that genes may have the immediate effect Holland describes as the basis and only clear use of the language of causation. But they do not act on their own initiative or alone. So even in such cases Bowker prefers to talk of constraints rather than causes:

What is required is an adequate specification or description of the underlying constraints which have, with some immediacy, brought about the phenomenon to be explained.[19]

His 'with some immediacy' simply implies that one may never be able to make a list, all the way back, of all relevant constraints (but it is not clear why all the constraints should be 'underlying'). What Bowker advocates here is almost the reverse side of Popper's description. Where Popper viewed the positive possibilities and propensities as jostling to come into being, Bowker draws attention to the negative constraints which make it more difficult for any possibility to become one (as opposed to zero).

But he correctly says that constraints need not be regarded as negative; rather, they are a condition of freedom when they can be used constructively. He quotes Ashby on the development of cybernetics: 'Where a constraint exists, advantage can usually be taken of it.'[20] That may be an unduly optimistic account, given the narrowing, diminishing nature of some constraints in, for instance, poverty or disease. But it remains the case that genes are not machine-minders, initiating causal links in a determined chain. Rather they are part of the network of constraints within which all creatures, human and non-human, have to work, and by their very constraining they define the field of an organism's possibilities.

Dawkins wrote: 'It is all perfectly simple and delightfully automatic and unpremeditated.' That simplicity, however, comes from ignoring inputs other than genes into what takes place, while the process is automatic and machine-like only when the organism is abstracted from the network of constraints and possibilities within which it works. But it *is* unpremeditated as the beaver, or any other creature, explores a new possibility, and thus, in the theological framework, responds to God's letting-be.

2. Natural evil

The spacious firmament on high,
with all the blue ethereal sky,

And spangled heavens, a shining frame,
Their great Original proclaim.

Thus Addison, in a poem which is pure deism, but lingers in the
hymnbooks, celebrates the beauty, order and religious suggestive-
ness of the heavens. Others have found that response to mountains,
rivers or waterfalls. This is also a world of fascinating, endlessly
diverse, creatures. It is not surprising, then, that it should evoke
wonder and vivid appreciation from men and women. When these
sentiments are translated into 'green' theology they tend to be
summed up in the notion of goodness, appealing to the verses in
Genesis 1 where God pronounces creation good.

That in turn leads to a basic presumption of divinely derived
goodness in beauty or order in the world if only humanity would let it
alone. The call to human responsibility, in that case, is to maintain,
or restore, that initial goodness. Thus in *Man and Nature* the writers
express their faith 'that God created all things good, that he has
made man in his own image and that, despite the reality of sin, the
world and man essentially remain the good creation of God'.[21]

Again it is claimed that a good God would *necessarily* have created
a good world, one that would echo in its own way the divine
goodness:

Because God is the creator of the heavens and the earth and all
that is in them, creation is by definition good – even as God is
good.[22]

The senses of goodness applied to the created world in these
quotations appear to bridge notions of beauty, wholesomeness,
order and the reflection of moral rightness. To round out notions of
goodness one may add the sense of 'fitting' which some contemporary expositors of Genesis maintain, so that what God approved was
that everything was fitting together and achieving the role designed
for it.

There is no doubt that the beauty of the world, or the intricate way
in which creatures evolve and coexist, may arouse a sense of wonder
and thankfulness that such things should be. Nothing in this ensuing

argument denies that. But the question whether the world was created good, in any sense of either the verb or the adjective, is far too rarely addressed in theology concerned with the environment.

What is fundamentally surprising in the appeal to Genesis 1 is that it by-passes entirely all accounts of evolution. The six days of creation may not be so much at issue now, but from descriptions of goodness one would never know that Darwin wrote of the 'struggle for life'. Even where some consciousness of evolution exists, there may be facile accounts of God creating a good world down a time line, as if natural evil were not a problem.

The Creation is the invisible background of Evolution. Evolution is the visible foreground of Creation.[23]

Meye, on the other hand, the author of the second quotation given above, has no place for evolution at all, and simply brackets out the whole question of evil in the affirmation of the world's basic goodness:

Not the least of mysteries – perhaps the greatest of mysteries for the faith – is the fact of evil in the world.[24]

But to celebrate the goodness of creation while simply dismissing all contrary indications in evil as a mystery is neither intellectually nor religiously satisfying. In common with many other theologians, Meye is ready to describe the force of evil as human sin affecting all of creation, again following the pattern of Genesis. But human sin hardly accounts for hurricanes, nor for the suffering and disaster which had happened to creation before humanity appeared. Even in the consideration of evil we have been anthropocentric.

Moral evil occurs between human beings, and it has been taken as evidence of sin in intention or act. It has always been a problem, however, on the Genesis pattern, to say why sin should have been possible in God's good created world. Moreover, some of the suffering which human beings undergo cannot be accounted for as the results of their own, or of other human beings', wrong-doing. Such manifestations as tidal waves or earthquakes, therefore, were understood in a separate category of *natural* evil, which arose simply from the way the world is: 'something logically necessary within creation', as Fiddes says in criticism.[25]

Until very recently, however, most accounts of natural evil were concerned with the suffering of *human beings* from natural processes, but not with any suffering among other creatures. It was questioned, on a philosophical, rather than an empirical basis, whether non-humans could indeed suffer. If they could not, then nothing that could happen to them could possibly be called evil.[26] Thus cancer in human beings was a natural evil, but cancer in wild animals was negligible. An earthquake in which no human was killed was not considered evil, no matter how much panic, suffering or displacement arose in the natural world.

But sensibilities, and indeed moral arguments on this suffering in nature, have changed, a matter to which I shall return in discussing the moral standing of the non-human. What is relevant here is that if the disasters and suffering of the natural world are perceived to be worthy of moral consideration, then the question of God's responsibility for that suffering is raised. Thus, when *Man and Nature* considers the incidence of famine, plague, flood and so forth, the conclusion is:

> No doubt some of these matters belong to the unfinished state of creation and some to the conditions that necessarily belong to existence in an orderly physical universe, but there is a core which seems to place a question mark against the doctrine of creation by a loving God.[27]

The 'problem of evil' within the Christian faith has centred on how belief in the existence of a good and powerful God may be maintained in the midst of the viciousness, pain and suffering in the world. In environmental theology, that becomes the question whether God may be said to care for the natural world, given the amount of entirely natural suffering and species extinction within it. For if God does not care, there is no specifically *Christian* reason for being involved in saving species, preserving habitats or improving conditions.

I have already cited Brunner's vivid expression of the problem:

The more fully we ascribe – in our doctrine of creation – responsibility to God for that which is created, the more disturbing is our view of the actual reality of the world. Can this world, so full of meaninglessness, cruel suffering and death – be God's creation?[28]

In writing that, Brunner was probably thinking only of human suffering, so when suffering in the natural world is added, the accumulation is immense. He is right to calibrate the degree of disturbance to faith with the degree of responsibility attributed to God. But he never seriously answers his own question. A transcendent God who has shaped and ordered creation does bear resonsibility for, among other things, the climate change brought about, perhaps, by the dust from a meteor crash, which resulted in a massive extinction 65 million years ago, of which the demise of the dinosaurs is the best-known example.

Such a sovereign transcendent God must also have ordered the habits of some insects which lay their eggs inside other creatures so that the larvae may feed on their unwilling and still living hosts. Darwin mentioned the ichneumons in this regard:

> I cannot persuade myself that a beneficent and omnipotent God would have designedly created the Ichneumonidae with the express intention of their feeding within the living bodies of caterpillars.[29]

Stephen Jay Gould has followed the preoccupation with these flies in theodicy ever since, and the reluctance to allow their habits to tell against a morally responsible divine design, part of the 'goodness' of Genesis 1. He cites Julian Huxley in his support:

> Natural selection, in fact, though like the mills of God in grinding slowly and grinding small, has few other attributes that a civilized religion would call divine . . . Its products are just as likely to be aesthetically, morally, or intellectually repulsive as they are to be attractive. We need only think of the ugliness of *Sacculina* or a bladder worm, the stupidity of a rhinoceros or a stegosaur, the

horror of a female mantis devouring its mate or a brood of ichneuman flies slowly eating out a caterpillar.[30]

All that is a far cry from the beauty of creation which Keith Ward calls 'achievements of form and pattern which reveal, and are intended to reveal, the character of their ultimate cause as creative mind'.[31] Again one might ask what kind of creative mind is revealed by killer whales playing with seals before killing them, as cats play with mice. Alternatively, one might conclude that if these do reveal the creative mind of God, that mind is not one to be moved by non-human suffering. That was also the conclusion of Peter Geach:

> The Creator's mind, as manifested in the living world, seems to be characterized by mere indifference to the pain that the elaborate interlocking teleologies of life involve.[32]

Geach in fact argues that one should not attribute to God every human value. Chastity, for instance, may be a human value, but its attribution to God would be absurd. Sympathy, he suggests, might be equally inappropriate:

> God is not an animal as men are, and if he does not change his designs to avoid pain and suffering to animals he is not violating any natural sympathies.[33]

Long before Geach, David Hume had arrived at the same conclusion, namely, that if one were to begin from how the human or natural worlds were, one would conclude to an indifferent deity. In the natural world, for instance, there may be too much or too little of a good thing:

> Thus the winds are requisite to convey the vapours along the surface of the globe, and to assist men to navigation; but how often, rising up to tempests and hurricanes, do they become pernicious? Rains are necessary to nourish the plants and animals of the earth; but how often are they defective? how often excessive? Heat is requisite to all life and vegetation, but is not always found in the due proportion.[34]

His unavoidable conclusion is:

> that the original source of all things is entirely indifferent . . . and
> has no more regard to good above ill than to heat above cold, or to
> drought above moisture, or to light above heavy.[35]

Hume was opposing the deist argument to the existence of God
from the manifestations of design (order, goodness) in the world.
His conclusion in relation to that empirical argument seems
inescapable. There simply is not that unambiguous goodness, at
least as humans understand the term, in the natural world. But his
chilling conclusion is equally relevant against another frequent
theological move concerning natural evil, namely that individual
evils serve a greater good.

That optimistic view of the totality, whatever misadventures
happen *en route*, has been with theology for a long time. Plato
believed that God, out of divine goodness, created every creature
possible. Later all these were arranged hierarchically into a great
Chain of Being. That rational picture allowed that among all these
creatures there would be some which would be incompatible and
conflict, but it was the goodness of the total pattern which counted.
No wonder, then, that Lovejoy could say that the God the pattern
revealed 'loved abundance and variety of life more than he loved
peace and concord among his creatures, and more than he desired
their exemption from pain'.[36]

Such optimism is not confined to believers in the great Chain of
Being. It occurs whenever a greater good is held to outweigh all
instances of suffering in the natural world. Holmes Rolston, for
instance, who is quite clear that all life that resists entropy has value,
still describes ecosystems as good in their *process*, whatever disasters
may occur to their individual members.[37] Although Rolston is not
himself putting forward a theodicy, if his emphases were to be
followed, there would simply be a change from the Great Chain of
Being in a static hierarchy to a Great Process of Becoming in
dynamic ecosystems as the totality in relation to which individual
disasters are negligible.

A different kind of pattern is provided by those who believe that the processes of the world are there to lead to humanity's arrival, and if there are some accidents on the way, like intermittent massive extinctions, that is incidental because humanity did at last arrive. Brian Hebblethwaite, for instance, is one of many who believe the process was designed to lead to 'genuinely automonous agents' (although that description of humanity is itself debatable), for whom God has, through the history of evolution, provided a base in the creatures of the natural world:

> But such a process, and such creatures are bound to be at risk of occasional clashes.[38]

Arthur Peacocke similarly values highly 'persons making free decisions'. He argues that pain, fragility and vulnerability are inevitable aspects of a material universe, and that new life on earth can only arise through death. I would not dissent from any of that, but I would from his conclusion:

> It seems hard to avoid the paradox that 'natural evil' is a necessary prerequisite for the emergence of free, self-conscious beings.[39]

That seems to make it all right. Indeed Peacocke describes natural evil as the random elements 'which come to man'; suffering which does not come to man is not even considered.

The cavalier approach to the natural world evident in the last two paragraphs could have been taken only by men who did not believe nature to have any significance of its own to God, or any part in the divine purposes except as means to a human end. These have been quite normal attitudes among Christian theologians until the ecological crisis awoke us from our dogmatic slumbers – almost too late. They still describe an indifferent God, this time a God who has been indifferent over the millennia of evolving creation to everything that did not contribute to humanity's arrival, and even for that evolutionary pathway was only mildly interested until humanity arrived.

That belief has been backed up by a view of love as possible only when it may be returned. As such love is thought of in human terms, only human beings are able to return love, and thus creation was vacuous to God, and God to creation until humanity appeared. In this vein Brunner argued that 'love can only impart itself where it is received in love'.[40] The consequences of such limitation put on love, as if no one had ever loved unrequitedly, and as if human love were an adequate yardstick for divine love, are made devastatingly clear by John Dickie:

> The world exists for our sakes, and not for its own. This follows from the truth that it is only personal beings capable of responding to Love that can be objects of Love in the true meaning of the term. God wills the world, therefore, as a means, but only as a means.[41]

The impact such beliefs, or lack of beliefs, have had on humanity's relationships with, and behaviour towards, the natural world could be extensively documented. Here, as a brief example, it may be said that one could agree with Peacocke that death is natural while new life will not find a niche without it. But that is true of humanity as well, and we treat that kind of death with respect, not only because this is one of our own species, but also because the human who died is valuable to God. If similar respect had been given to the death of animals understood to be the objects of divine love, within the Christian faith, it would have been far more difficult for some callous industrial farming and abattoir practices to develop.

The ecological crisis raises another point against those teleologies which devalue the process in order to celebrate the arrival of free autonomous agents at the end. Humanity is not, in fact, such a success story as to have been the point of it all. We have thoughtlessly destroyed, polluted and exhausted whole swathes of country and creatures. Our intelligence and technological abilities have proved a very two-edged sword. It is precisely the sense of the superiority of humanity over the rest, implicit in Peacocke and Hebblethwaite, Brunner and Dickie, that has led to the behaviour which gave rise to the ecological crisis. Even if the planet were, as Hebblethwaite suggests, only our base, it is one humans have wantonly mishandled. If indeed we are what God was aiming at in physical creation, we must be even more of a disappointment than traditional theology suggests, for we must add excess and spoliation to our sins.

Against all devaluing of individual suffering by placing it against some large pattern held to be good in itself, I wish to argue that to God, and hence to Christians in general and theologians in particular, the suffering of individual creatures of all kinds matters. Just as individual humans matter to God, so do individual non-humans. God is not a distant maker of tidy patterns in whose process some will suffer, like eggs being broken for an omelette, but rather God is endlessly, steadfastly accompanying every part of creation in its joyful living and painful experience.

A far more positive relationship with the natural world is shown by Austin Farrer:

> Every sparrow is its own little self; it is no mere complex of general principles in combined action.[42]

Moreover, Farrer's God is far from indifferent to anything in creation. He argues that it is true of God with both human and non-human creation that:

> God does not need the compulsive pinch of sympathetic pain to make him do us good, his attitude is of a continual well-wishing expressed in continual well-doing.[43]

Farrer, in the same Platonizing manner as Ward, believes that God *thinks* creatures into being, but thereafter, Farrer holds, 'he makes them follow their own bent and work out the world by being themselves'.[44] In language reminiscent of process theology Farrer argues that God 'persuades' the creatures; God 'fosters' them and uses 'creative pressure' of which they are not aware for the satisfaction of individual lives and for evolution to continue.

Process theologians likewise, for whom God is immanently involved rather than distantly designing, still hold that God has given all creatures an 'initial aim', and 'lures' them on to fulfil this, although they are free to go their own way. The initial aim is a divinely-given impulse to a creature 'to actualize the best possibility open to it, given its concrete situation'.[45]

But God does not control the situation, so the subject is free to choose from other possibilities open to it. That is the risk God takes, and the inferior choices are the source of evil in the world:

> The obvious point is that, since God is not in complete control of the events of the world, the occurrence of general evil is not incompatible with God's beneficence toward all his creatures.[46]

Farrer likewise finds no theological difficulty in natural evil, since that is just what would happen in a world where creatures are free.

> [God] does not let natural forces have their heads up to the point only at which their free action would conflict with some fixed principle of higher purpose.[47]

Farrer believes that God may work the evil into good, although it is not clear how this happens; but an earthquake, for instance, is a practical problem: 'no theological problem arises'.

There is much in these accounts with which I would agree. If God gives creation freedom to respond to possibility as it can, there will be, in its multiplicity and over time, clashes and conflict in that response. Tectonic plates that developed at one time in that freedom will later cause earthquakes, and probable suffering. Similarly, food chains and the distressing (to human beings) habits of certain creatures are the ways in which possibilities and constraints in genes and environment have been developed. In that sense there is no theological problem, and no bar to God's loving companionship of the way things are now.

But that explanation does not remove humanity from the need for compassion, any more than natural evils which can be explained on scientific grounds remove compassion from the humans who suffer them. I am not suggesting that the *same* sorrow or fellow-feeling occurs when, say, birds die in a hurricane and when a human being dies. But all the deaths are part of the tragedy, and because all life is worthy of respect, there would be tragedy even if no human lives were lost.

Although this discussion concerns natural evil, the evil arising from natural processes, it should also be acknowledged that the recognition of value to God in the natural world enlarges the scope of *moral* evil as well in the possibility of mistreatment of the natural world by human beings in, for instance, the discharge from a tanker covering birds in oil, making it impossible for them to fly, or effluent from a factory killing fish. The change in sensibility to greater *human* valuing of the natural world is most evident in indignation at just such malpractices, and the theological justification for the outcry lies in affirming that such lives do indeed matter to God.

It is one thing, however, to say that lives *matter* to God, and another to say whether God is in any direct or indirect sense *responsible* for how they are and what difficulties they face. Farrer and process theologians are clear that nature directs its own course (and so may produce evil), but they retain a place for God's action in persuading, luring, 'making the creatures make themselves' (Farrer). Such language, if it is to be used at all, has to be used carefully, for it has problems of its own in relation to the history of evolution.

According to some accounts of process theology God gives an impulse, an 'initial aim' towards the current best possibility, although the creature is otherwise free. Yet there are also statements which appear to restrict creation's freedom more tightly in the name of creative advance towards complexification, and hence more intense enjoyment, further on in evolution. Thus Hartshorne writes of limits set to free decisions 'mitigating the risk and maximizing the promise of freedom'.[48] Again, Pailin, with the processes of evolution in mind, writes:

> God's creative activity . . . is to be conceived as ensuring that the constituents of reality belong to a process which combines stability with an appropriate degree of openness to novelty, and which contains an intrinsic urge towards combination in increasingly complex patterns.[49]

On the one hand, then, for process theologians, there is God urging on to complexification, but on the other, it is worth noting that well over 90% of all the species that have ever been had become extinct, even before lethal humanity came on the scene. It would seem, then, that the divine lure and creative activity were considerably less than effective. While numbers are not everything, the scale of loss is impressive.

> During brief intervals mass extinctions have eliminated large numbers of species – sometimes most of the species on earth – on a global geographic scale.[50]

Such matters as continental drift, ocean circulation, the level of seas relative to land surfaces and climatic patterns have all played their part. There is not much evidence of the success of the divine lure in the overall picture.

It is possible, however, that this is again a piece of human triumphalism writ large over evolutionary history. At the time of the dinosaurs our mammal ancestor was a tiny shrew-like creature. With the dinosaurs out of the way, however, mammals developed remarkably in many directions, finally producing *homo sapiens*. That is the only piece of evolutionary history which really fits the pattern of process theology. And we are back to the indifferent God, careless of wastage and the conditions leading to extinction of the rest, so that the failure of the lure in all directions save one scarcely matters.

Two things in the doctrine I have been proposing would circumvent that unhappy conclusion. The first concerns the kind of action in which God engages. The language of fostering, luring, making creatures make themselves while mitigating the risks involved reveals the last glimmer of the 'God who acts', shaping creation, if only creation would let itself be shaped. I have not suggested any such programme on God's part, although God undoubtedly has desires for how creation goes. But these desires for freedom and love give a character to the divine side of the relationship which has no directing hidden agenda. Process theology certainly works in terms of God's relatedness to creation, indeed essential (not chosen) relatedness, but that has more to do with connection than with the fullness of relationship I described earlier.

The other part of the doctrine which works with that relationship is that teleology is always now! It is with creatures as they live, rather than persuading them further up the evolutionary ladder. Indeed there is no ladder, a metaphor which gives comfort to human beings at the top. Instead, there is only diversity with different skills and lives. Creatures that have endured in simple form show how environmentally fit they have been and still are. The environmental fitness of humans is far less demonstrable. Again, creatures who die in the recurrent ice ages, or who are caught in the lava from volcanoes, have their importance to God, and their relation with God during their lives. In that case, neither continuing background extinction, nor the devastation of species in cataclysms, tells against God's companionship and possibilities of influence in the world.

Much of the shape of this book has derived from my firm conviction that everything that happens in the natural world, including its suffering, and its mistreatment by humans, matters to God. I cannot imagine it possible to worship a God responsible for natural evil any more than one responsible for moral evil. The knock-on effects of that conviction have been worked out primarily in the areas of what God may be believed to create and do, and where the teleological thrust lies. To those who wish to affirm full-blooded (so to speak) making and doing, this version will appear anaemic. But the consequences of belief in a more virile God, who has to be responsible for the removal of around 98% of all species ever, but who fails to do anything in millions of cases of acute suffering in nature and humanity, are scarcely to be borne.

Yet even this version does not entirely overcome the problem, and Farrer was perhaps too optimistic in saying no theological problem remained. In my case, it could be argued that God, in creating possibility, should have been able to conceive of its being used differently by different creatures, thus giving rise to the kinds of circumstances summed up as evil. The only way to offset that conclusion is to look for a greater good gained even through the difficulties, and that is a move that I have already criticized. But my criticism was directed against notions of a greater good which implicitly *devalued* the suffering. If God accompanies all creatures through suffering as well as in the good times, that suffering is not devalued, but becomes rather part of the risk and cost of the good that is possible.

Charles Raven expresses the series of consequences thus, and what he writes of selfhood is applicable, not only to humans, but to every kind of creaturely self:

> It begins to look as if the possibility of disobedience was the price of liberty, just as liberty is the condition of selfhood, and selfhood the preliminary to fellowship.[51]

Fellowship, concurrence or relationship among creatures and between creatures and God is the greatest good of creation. The possibility of such relationships is what creation is about. But, as Raven writes, it takes selves to enter into fellowship, and freedom to develop into selves. That freedom may produce the disobedience he suggests, a term fit for human beings, or, more simply, human and non-human suffering from the way in which change and variety in creation have unpredictable and unfortunate results. If God viewed the process from afar, the charge of indifference would remain. But precisely because God is involved in the relationships, the pain as well as the pleasure is part of the divine experience. Yet it cannot be relieved by God, since that would remove the fundamental freedom to use possibility, which is the gift of creation. But humans do not have this constraint, since they did not grant freedom in the first place. Moreover, being creatures themselves, whatever they do will bring about changes in the created world. Therefore they, unlike God, may work to avoid or alleviate the pains of natural evil where they can.

3. Is anthropocentricity inescapable?

In the last section I pointed out various ways in which theological argument had overlooked or underplayed the importance to both God and human beings of non-human creation as it is, without reference to humanity's needs. The charge of anthropocentrism, of being concerned from first to last with the character and status of humanity, is one that has regularly, and with some justice, been levelled against Christianity since Lynn White first blamed that characteristic for fuelling the ecological crisis.[52] That has led to considerable revaluation and reweighting in theology. Necessary as such response is, however, it is a genuine question whether anthropocentricity may ever be wholly avoided by men and women in their relations to what is not human. But then, if it is inescapable, how does such self-awareness figure in an environmentally-concerned doctrine of creation?

Keith Tester argues that human concern over animal welfare or rights never ceases to be a concern over *human* identity just as much as previous ill-treatment was. Humans manipulate animals into being reference points for their own self-understanding.

> Animals are only made the site of moral concern to the extent that they are useful in establishing social definitions of the properly human.[53]

Even those who plead for animal rights are appealing precisely to the moral conscience and the intelligence of human beings concerning animals who lack these superior features. Moreover, the calls for concern over animal welfare are more likely to be heard by those in cities who experience no threat to life or livelihood from animals, and are thus not concerned to demonstrate their difference and superiority with force. That force, however, remains, even for the urbanized, in the way animals become food or clothing.

Tester writes in a superior, debunking tone, as if having shown the humanness of a human concern were enough to explode its rationale or sensitivity. Nevertheless, his point is worth consideration. Equally worthy of consideration is the more measured argument of Robin Grove-White, that the success of the Green movement is indicative of a dissatisfaction in society over both the political trivialization of the public's role in society and the negative effects perceived in the inflated role of science and technology. The sense of who a person is has now been diminished and disempowered, while the official version of the crisis and its individual problems ignores that dimension entirely.

Orthodoxy defines the environmental crisis as a set of identifiable physical problems, some of them acknowledged as deep-rooted in our economic practice and very difficult to address. 'Solving' the most intractable of them, it is suggested, will require major achievements of regulation, fiscal innovation and international diplomacy, as well as goodwill of a kind almost without precedent.[54]

Grove-White, who spent almost two decades as an environmental campaigner, would not deny that analysis. But his point is that the issue is more than a series of individual physical problems. The success of groups like Friends of the Earth or Greenpeace come from having focussed public concern since the 1970s on such issues as 'the soaring trajectories of industrial society', or 'the inadequacy of present regulatory processes for controlling rampant consumption' (17). Yet:

How and why 'the public' (reflected in the NGOs) understood the issues in advance of the arrival of official 'science', or why 'intuitions' should have resonated so powerfully with wider social attitudes, is not considered a matter of significance, and these days tends to be set aside in official circles (18).

The expectation that there will be purely scientific answers, moreover, is defeated by the perception that *environmental* science, which is conducted in the real world, in non-laboratory conditions, is unable to give certainty. The variables involved in these circumstances on any issue are virtually infinite, while politics, society and the questions being raised are also all in flux.

This helps explain why it is that controversy is so recurrent in politically sensitive fields in which science is used by official environmental agencies to underwrite action or to provide political reassurance (19).

The environmental agenda, therefore, is hedged about with uncertainty and double meaning. Arguments about pesticide use, for instance, certainly concern issues of safety, but also

> challenge the arrogance and reductionism of the regulators' and official scientific advisers' unilateral assumptions about human behaviour in real world situations (28).

Scientific answers from on high are thus no longer simply to be accepted, because what they imply concerning human being is no longer acceptable, and that unease finds its focus in environmental protest.

> There are good reasons why 'the environment' has come to play this role – not the least of them being its previously 'uncolonized' character as a political/ideological domain, and the role of the nature/man, science/politics dualism as a central, structural tension in Western thought (30).

There is thus a case for believing that expressions of concern for what is not human at the same time express a concern for what it is to be human. Tester uses words like 'simply', 'merely', 'just' for the explanation of concern about animals being a social problem of identity. While his argument has point, it becomes, in these terms, a sociological reduction of human behaviour. There is, certainly, a human shape to relations with, say, pets and farm animals, and the arguments over fox-hunting may be seen as much in terms of what human beings are like as of what is good for a wild animal.

This is a limitation of finitude, and puts human beings back among other creatures, who, presumably, interpret their environment in their own terms. I am certain that my local robin regards me as an inefficient digger up of worms. In ecological terms, any organism explores its environment for its useful features, and human beings with their conceptual capacities explore it conceptually as well as materially. We may transcend the natural world in having such capacities, but we are embedded in it in the way we use them. Only God, I have already suggested, can know and transcend the experience of all species without being limited by species-specific interpretation.

There is also a valid point to be extracted from Tester's case that knowing who one is also involves knowing who one is not. The history of human relations with non-human beings, which Tester relates, shows how the latter have been manipulated in the not-human category to make a clear demarcation line. Human beings are not beasts. This thinking can still appear in some surprising situations. Thus Hans Küng, appealing to the *humanum* as a basic ecumenical criterion, writes:

> What is human, truly human, what has human dignity, can with justification appeal to the 'divine'. But what is inhuman, 'animal', 'bestial', cannot with justification appeal to the 'divine'.[55]

Certainly Küng uses quotation marks, and has a particular sense of the 'divine' here, but this instance shows how animals continue to serve human beings as their conceptual opposites. The pity is that that the demarcation line has resulted in a lack of respect and consideration for what falls on the not-human side.

But that again has much in common with other boundaries in human identity-recognition. When Social Darwinism was in force, for instance, there was a conceptual boundary between developed white races and all others, who were believed to be little more than beasts and needed to be treated like children. That attitude, and the belief that underpinned it, have gone, although racism persists. That shows that boundaries may be rethought as society moves on, but not in a uniform manner. In this case, the boundary markers between what is human and what may be found in other species – intelligence, tool-use, language – are much less clear as understanding increases. It remains to be seen whether humans can live with the ambiguity of being both a part of nature and apart from nature.

The form human anxiety takes, as Grove-White describes it, suggests that this conception of the dual status of humanity is already held, at least among those dedicated to green issues. He sees that it is precisely features of the human, all-too-human, society in economics, politics and science which are felt to be constricting to human being, so that people turn to the more open, relational, responsible way of being which they find in green movements. People do this using human, social terms and concepts. Of course, it cannot be otherwise, since that is all the language we have. But the increasing numbers world-wide moved by such issues do wish to include a positive, thoughtful, unselfish relationship with the natural world as part of what it is to be human.

Jonathon Porritt would agree with Grove-White that environmental concern indicates a deep human malaise. He quotes Neil Evernden with approval:

> For although they seldom recognize it, environmentalists are protesting not at the stripping of natural resources, but the stripping of earthly meaning.

However, for Porritt the malaise is not only societal, it has spiritual roots.

> I think we can still discern today an enormous need for some kind of spiritual fulfilment and spiritual meaning, a need to look beyond the material confines within which most of our life is pitched. It's difficult to pin down: dogmatize that kind of feeling, try and classify it, try and pigeonhole it by putting a bit of pretentious polysyllabic nomenclature to it, and it just blows away. Theologians don't like this, but this kind of spiritual yearning is not so much an intellectual abstraction as a powerfully felt gut-feeling, a metaphorical throb of the heart.[56]

Before summing up what all this implies for human anthropocentricity, a further subtle, anthropic character of linguistic description deserves consideration. Gillian Beer has approached Darwin's *Origin of Species* as a literary critic, concerned with the reach of language. The *Origin* is full of descriptions (stories) and metaphors to assist the imaginative reordering of experience that the book required. She notes the capacity of the overarching story to become, not one, but many different myths, of 'the struggle for life', or 'natural selection', by which humans understood themselves. But that took the story far beyond what Darwin had intended.

His text has a progenitive power. He seeks to express the equivalence of man with all other forms of life, but the power of his writing and the novelty of his language make it appear that Darwin, man's representative, has as much created as described.[57]

Other writers on the environment use something of the wealth of stories and imaginative appeal of Darwin, and they are creating narratives, a very human act. Television programmes, like David Attenborough's *Trials of Life*, have the same myth-making potential, aided by the vividness of film. These are the narratives which shape the often inchoate spiritual yearning Porritt describes.

From all this it appears that the capacity to transcend human language, conceptualization and concerns is strictly limited. In relation to what is not human, or has not been made by humans, our powers of comprehension are limited and are bound to reflect their human and social origin. That, as I point out from time to time, has long been recognized in connection with language about God, the 'wholly other' of whom we still speak out of the religious tradition and present experience. But now, the new situation is that the same limitation has to be recognized with regard to species and their systems other than our own. To know the world from another species' point of view is beyond us, although sympathetic imagination may help to bridge that gap. Human language and experience are the sources of both our opportunities and our limitations, our possibilities and our constraints.

Given that inescapable degree of anthropocentrism, however, there is a clear difference between those who are happy to remain with human issues as being all that human beings should be concerned about, and those whose consciousness is raised by the conditions (humanly understood) of other species. Peter Singer, for example, in *Animal Liberation*, draws attention to the *suffering* of animals, and argues that they have *interests*.[58] The suffering and interests may be understood *by analogy with our own*, with the difference of no foresight, we think, in animals. Thus the *range* of human compassion is enlarged, and animals will, apart from human ineptitude, profit from that. Their possibilities, so important in this doctrine of creation, will be enhanced.

The difference in attitude was graphically illustrated in a recent television programme, and the role of television in changing attitudes can hardly be overestimated. In this case, instead of breaking in horses by creating fear in them and exercising mastery over them, a trainer had studied the movements, the 'language' of horses, and in half an hour could break in (the wrong verb in his case) a horse by using its language movements and making friends with it. This still meant in the end that the human being had control, but the means used, and the attitude to a horse it displayed, were utterly different from the masterful anthropocentricity of the traditional practices. It is surely part of a doctrine of creation to describe a world in relation to God where such understanding behaviour would be the norm.

Lynn White blamed Christianity for its anthropocentricity, but Robin Grove-White has a different question for the faith:

> Does Christian insight about the nature of 'the person' have anything distinctive to tell the world about the phenomenon of environmental crisis and concern?[59]

That is the question to which we come next, with some critical examination of the past, and some desire, in spite of the theological language which Porritt distrusts, to express Christian possibilities from the spiritual quest of environmentalists.

4. Human and non-human: the image of God

The creation of humanity as it is described in Genesis 1.26–28 is an event attended by a description (image of God) and a function (dominion) quite unlike anything given to any other creature. It is not surprising, then, that although image-of-God language is rare in the Old Testament, and refers to Christ in the New (e.g. Col.1.15), the term came to focus for men and women what is special about human creatures and different from all other species. But exactly *what* is held to be special about humans has varied at different times in the tradition.

When Milton in *Paradise Lost* Book IV described Adam as 'like God erect', he was using one of the traditional distinctions made. No other creature stood on its hind legs; God was thought of in personal terms, and hence erect. So humanity was a physical image. 'The bodily image,' says von Rad, commenting on this verse, 'is not to be split off from the spiritual' since the whole 'man' is created in the image.[60] But in the history of doctrine that very split, with its implicit downgrading of the physical, occurred.

Far more important than physical imaging, however, was the location of the image of God in some human capacity which marked its bearer off from all other creatures. To the intelligent, learned theologians who pondered this question it was clear that human reason provided the distinguishing feature. But this attribution was not simply a celebration of humans as 'thinking animals' (Aristotle), for by reason rational creatures could seek out God's thoughts and discern good and evil.

The modern conception of human intelligence as that which may discern the divine mind in the laws of physics, or in the first moments of cosmic history, is in the same tradition. Indeed human capacity in this, as in other intellectual fields, is formidable. Yet, now as then, mind becomes important at the expense of body, and reason at the expense of relationship or sensitivity. The body with its feeling has instead often been seen as what held men back, inhibiting the rational freedom to think and make decisions, which was the divine endowment. But when the emphasis changes to one of relationship the body regains its importance in visibly expressing that relationship, although it no longer is understood as echoing God in its upright stance.

The body is not a discardable garment cloaking the real self or essence of a person (or a pine tree or a chimpanzee); rather it is the shape or form of who we are. It is how each of us is recognized, responded to, loved, touched, and cared for – as well as oppressed, beaten, raped, mutilated, discarded, and killed.[61]

Reason, indeed, as the locus of the image of God, was not only artificially divorced from all the rest that goes to make up the human, it also tended to be celebrated as a positive characteristic, playing down the intentional or unintentional evil that a 'meddling intellect' can do. In the end it is true of all candidates for what constitutes the image of God, if that is considered to be a human endowment, that human ambiguity renders them doubtful. Any present use of the image, therefore, will have to be more subtle.

In the nineteenth century, reason's relationship with theology became more complicated as science took over the definition of what reason was. Other human capacities were then advanced for the divine image – moral nature, creativity, personhood itself. What remained constant in all these descriptions was that they should distinguish clearly the superiority of human beings over the rest of creation, and humanity's likeness to God.

> The beasts are not so. They are not moral, nor responsible, not disengaged from material circumstance; not true causes. Man is all this, and so can know God as like knows like. God, the Archetype of all Personality, supremely self-conscious, self-acting, moral, has made man to be, in the remarkable words of the Apocrypha, 'the image of his own peculiar nature' (Wisdom 2.3).[62]

A different emphasis concerning the image comes out in Barth and Brunner, who, in their different ways, describe it in terms of a certain kind of *relationship* with God rather than as a divinely-given ontology. There had long been a difference of opinion in theology over whether the image of God persisted (and, if so, to what degree) after the Fall. The optimists invoked the incarnation to argue that human being was good enough for the Son of God. The pessimists retorted that human being was bad enough to *need* the Son of God. As regards the natural human state, Barth and Brunner are both pessimists. The image of God, Barth writes, 'is not a quality in man'. Yet Barth retains the term because God desires a creature, which in all of its non-deity and therefore its differentiation can be a real partner; which is capable of action and responsibility in relation to him; to which his own divine form of life is not alien.[63]

Brunner likewise emphasizes responsiveness and responsibility as something only humans have.

The animals, and God, have no responsibility – the animals because they are below the level of responsibility, and God, because he is above it; the animals because they have no freedom, and God because he has absolute freedom. Man, however, has a limited freedom . . . he possesses *this* freedom in order that he may respond to God, in such a way that through this response God may glorify himself, and give himself to his creature.[64]

Thus for Barth and Brunner only humans-in-relation-to-God, not humans-as-humans reflect the divine glory in which, for them, the image consists. The difference from non-human nature remains. Human responsibility looms large, although one may wonder at Brunner's absolution of God from any, since in his scheme God permitted human beings their vulnerable freedom in the first place. It remains a human possibility to obstruct the divine reflection by sin, and 'it is this which differentiates man from the lower creation'.[65]

Douglas John Hall, in his *Imaging God*, takes this sense of relationship right into the throes of the ecological crisis.[66] As his title suggests, his emphasis is less on the noun 'image' as an endowment of humanity than on the *activity* of imaging within the relationship. In this move from ontology to action he reflects what many Old Testament scholars believe about Genesis 1.26. The basis of the metaphor of 'image' has been considered to be the habit of a conqueror or governor to have his statue placed in his far-flung dominions to remind the local people who ruled there.

Even among biblical scholars who agree on the basis of the metaphor in a statue, however, the force of the image has changed since awareness of the ecological crisis. Von Rad in the 1960s is forthright on the task the gift implies: 'domination in the world, especially over animals'.[67] However gently or powerfully human dominion is expressed, however, on this reading the statue is there to fulfil a function, and so is humanity. A current interpretation, therefore, which is less harsh than von Rad's, is that God in Genesis 1 has just made an orderly, 'good' creation, which men and women, imaging God, are to maintain in that order and goodness.

That is no exaltation of humanity. Gibson, for instance, in his commentary, remarks on the overwhelmingly low estimate of humanity in the Old Testament, which is not likely to be overturned in this passage.[68] What humanity is capable of, according to Gibson, is some understanding of what God was about in creation, and so may preserve its perfection. But the question is whether this was ever a real possibility. Many exegetes believe that the Priestly Writer of Genesis, at the end of the sixth century BCE, was describing, even at the time of writing, what he thought would be an *ideal* social and ecological paradise under God as a comparison with the inferior conditions of his own day.[69]

Hall picks up the theme of activity, and continues the emphasis on relationship, within which that activity takes on the characteristics of a vocation. The calling he describes as being-in-relationship. Rationality, personhood and all the other valued attributes in the history of the doctrine are the means to the end of establishing and maintaining the relationship. Expressed in ontological terms, what Hall envisages is not humanity as being, but humanity as being-with (Heidegger's *Mitsein* again), which includes a being-for and a being-together. In other language, authentic humanity *is* co-existence, pro-existence and community. Inauthentic humanity is disclosed in being-alone (autonomy), being-against (alienation), being-above (pride), being-below (sloth and the refusal of responsibility; Hall is not thinking of the poor and marginalized here).

But with whom is this *Mitsein*?

We name, then, three dimensions of human relatedness. The human being is being-with-God, who is source and ground of all being; it is being with the human counterpart . . . ; and it is being-with-nature. Humanity in God's intention means existing in dynamic, harmonious relationships with these three counterparts of our being. To be *imago Dei* implies that, standing within the relationship with God, the human creature reflects God's vicarious and gracious *Mitsein* in its life vis-à-vis these others.[70]

In this reimaging of the relationship, Hall has moved some distance from Barth and the Reformers, whom he cites as originating the relational concept. What is common to all the earlier versions is a concept of God as transcendent sovereign, absolute master of the relationship. Barth, for instance, while warmly aware that God will not abandon that finite and sinful creature 'man', is simultaneously driven to describe God as:

> the true and genuine Lord and King and Lawgiver and the sole Ruler of the creature by his Holy Spirit, who does not strike down but raises up, who does not bind but looses, who does not kill but makes alive.[71]

I have argued elsewhere that such a conception makes for an inadequate sense of relationship by today's standards.[72] It is autocratic, top-down, sets no intrinsic value on the creature, and reflects what would now be regarded as the very worst of human management styles, let alone relationships. The God whom Hall describes, while still transcendent and principally located somewhere other than creation, is less paradoxically expressed, so that it is the divine *Mitsein*, even from transcendence, which is the chief characteristic.

Hall explores sensitively human being with God, and human solidarity with the natural world. He bridges what is often thought of as an ontological-functional divide with his 'ontology of communion' which is also a vocation. But in one way he remains firmly within the tradition: human beings are still the pivot of the whole set of relationships. God's being-with the natural world is not explored as God's being-with humanity is. Humanity instead reflects God to the natural world. Little is made of what there might be in the natural world for God to value in the relationship. Again, while humans may be-with the natural world, rejecting notions of superiority, what does the natural world offer humans? A tricky question implicit in his argument is not addressed:

> If non-human creation has relational capacity, does this mean that it, too, images God? If so, then where does the distinction between human and non-human really lie?[73]

More, therefore, has to be said on the asymmetrical mutuality between God and humans, God and nature, humans and nature, requiring a reinterpretation even of the relational model.

The dangers of hubris, hyper-distinction and individualism in the developed theological traditions of the image of God are so great that there would be good reason for abandoning the language altogether in an ecologically-aware age. Yet human beings are intelligent and adaptable enough to have made a tremendous impact for both better and worse on the planet in a small amount of evolutionary time, and there are strands in the tradition which may be brought out to celebrate and lament these capacities, so long as humans are not seen to be acting in the *absence* of God, a notion apparently implicit in the original text, nor without the gifts of a natural world which could survive happily enough without them.

At the base of the whole argument in this book lies God's *Gelassenheit* in freedom and *Mitsein* in love. But that divine being-with in otherness and intimacy is always total, since God's character is not diluted according to species, although the divine understanding is itself species-specific. Moreover the relationship exists for *all* creation, not simply for the recently-arrived *homo sapiens*. If God can accommodate in relationship the infinite qualitative distinction between the divine and the human, there is not much more to ask of the divine in accommodating the rest of creation. The mutuality of God's participation here is the basis of the fulfilment of God's free and loving desire for instances of freedom and love, as far as these can be manifested in all the varieties of creatures with their genetic inheritance and changing, ambiguous circumstances.

While I wish to affirm the mutuality of the nature-God, nature-human relationship, there remains the impossibility of finding human words which are adequate to the natural world on its own terms, beyond what humans can make of its structure and behaviour in, say, Darwinian modes. On the one hand, because of the personal metaphors used of *God* one may, with due caution, speak of *divine* freedom and love on the basis of human understanding of these qualities. But, on the other hand, what would be freedom and love among the creatures of the natural world? May a word like 'love' be used of the response of a dung beetle? Or anywhere else in the natural world?

Freedom is a word that appears to make some sense in relation to creaturely exploration of the environment, which will certainly be a freedom within constraints of the possible in relation to other creatures. But then that is true of human freedom also. However, love is a far more humanly loaded term, and is thus restrictive in this wider context. Indeed, I have already described the way in which non-human incapacity to love as human beings do has been thought reason enough to exclude them from the divine purposes altogether.[74]

If one cannot credit a jellyfish or a crocodile with 'love' in anything like the sense human beings know it, but there still is to be something in all creaturely life which matters, and may be the basis of relationship between nature and God, perhaps 'appreciation of life' may be a phrase with suitable connotations. It is out of this appreciation that creatures use their possibilities, resist death and create their world. And since God has the whole gamut of appropriate understanding, God may be said to have co-appreciation of life as well as love. Moreover, God's is not that self-seeking kind of love which requires reciprocation in kind before it can continue, for in that case, even humans would not be able to qualify. In any case, what is proposed here for God's companionship of the world (pansyntheism) is that there is a relation between every creature and God analogous, in its own conditions, to one of love where human beings are concerned.

What I wish to propose now is that this divine–nature relationship makes possible *the imaging of God in the natural as well as the human world*, in the concurrence of non-humans with God's desire for creation. God appreciates life, that result of possibilities acted on, looks for appreciation of life, and finds that in divine intimacy with all manner of creatures which resist entropy and death. Further, in relation to human beings, the natural world may speak volumes on what is possible with freedom and what appreciation of life may be. In that sense it may image God to human beings.

A vivid example of this occurs in the continued use of dogs in mountain rescue in Scotland, as St Bernards were used in Switzerland. To someone lying injured on the mountainside in the dark, the first image of salvation may be the friendly face of a dog. Moreover, examples from the natural world have regularly been used to image a nation, or a state, so it is not impossible to find an admittedly finite and temporary image of God when nature is seen to concur with God. What is required is the openness to experience expressed in George McDonald's hymn 'O Lord of life':

> Whatever wakes my heart and mind
> Thy presence is, my Lord.

The divine presence may be embodied, imaged, in *whatever* stirs the attention and wakes the heart. The final triple concurrence then becomes one of God, the natural world and the human world collaborating against the diminishing of freedom and the wanton destruction of the conditions for life. With the inclusion of human beings life indeed becomes a moral issue, which it was not for non-human creatures alone, in, for example, food chains.

But there is more to human beings than that, although it is a very ambiguous 'more'. Pope's mixed estimate, 'a being darkly wise and rudely great', in his *Essay on Man* remains relevant, if it can be separated from notions of the Great Chain of Being on which it was based:

> Created half to rise and half to fall;
> Great lord of all things, yet a prey to all;
> Sole judge of truth, in endless error hurled;
> The glory, jest and riddle of the world.[75]

Perhaps humanity is 'pest' now, as much as 'jest' – polluter and exploiter, greedy for profit and careless of consequences. Equally, humanity is a 'riddle', perhaps, in using advanced technology to solve problems, but creating a whole nest of new problems (the atomic bomb, pesticides) *en route*.

But still, and simultaneously, humanity remains 'the glory of the world' – self-conscious, highly articulate, for all the limits and obscurities of language, creating civilizations, cultures, sciences; a generalist species that can turn its hand or brain to almost anything. Above all, in this doctrine of creation, a woman or man is a creature capable of relationships with other human beings and with non-human beings, relations that attend to and respect the otherness of the other, that work to the increase of positive possibilities, that can regard the other with uncoercive love or appreciation of its life –even while managing, say, a forest or a farm. And in all these ways humans concur with, and hence image, God.

One further, understandable use of the concept of the image of God does not deny this conclusion. The phrase is used to keep people whom society might reject still within the human family. Thus it has been important to women that the image in Genesis includes women as well as men, while theological accounts of those with AIDS insist that those suffering are not abandoned by God, but are still in the divine image. It is a way of emphasizing human dignity for those whose selfhood as human beings is at risk. In such cases comparison with the natural world is not at issue, but comparison with 'normal' valuable humanity is.

In so far as this human dignity is thought to be a divine endowment of humanity, it is as dubious as any other attributed endowment, given the actual ambiguity of all human life. But in so far as it connotes in marginal situations the continuation of human possibility it is to be affirmed. It has also been described as a learning *process*:

> The Christian vision of the *Imago Dei* is an invitation and powerful appeal to work for what we are not yet, to grow towards a fuller, more authentic personal and communal life in order to enable this divine image to become more transparent.[76]

In the final analysis, then, what makes for an image of God is what reflects in its finite way the characteristics of God in relation to creation. There is nothing automatic about that, but it happens (teleology now!) whenever the created concurs with the Creator. What is different about humanity lies in the *degree* of its range, not in its *kind*. The Priestly Writer of Genesis 1 had no notion of our common descent through evolving nature. Yet humanity has this vast repertoire of possibilities – physical, moral, intellectual, technological, social – which give it far more possibility of concurrence with God, but equally the possibility of failing far more spectacularly.

5. Human and non-human: dominion?

Problems in the theological use of the Bible, and the varieties of such use, could be amply illustrated by an extended consideration of what has been written invoking Genesis 1 (even more than Genesis 2), before and after environmental awareness changed perceptions. Here it can briefly be said that in current writing there are, broadly speaking, three approaches. The conservatives retain as much as possible from the Genesis account, like the 'goodness' of creation, while keeping silent on what has been dropped or changed, like the time-scale. The 'middle of the road' writers, with more or less acknowledgment of what they are doing, reinterpret what now seems regrettable into what fits with the new perceptions. Thus Jay McDaniel, wishing to retain force from the creation narratives in the midst of today's understanding of the galaxy and evolution, writes:

> The most promising way for Christians to appropriate the biblical story is to take seriously the idea that there is a divine dream at work in creation.[77]

In this way the Bible for this group may still give 'vision' or 'principles'. The third group, the radicals, simply dismiss the text as having no relevance to present issues and discussions.

Some kind of 'faithfulness to Scripture' may be argued for in all these approaches, but each case made has to be subtle and more or less tenuous. Conservative faithfulness consists in keeping what still appears viable, and interpreting that degree of viability generously by not raising external questions, such as those posed by evolution. The radicals leave the text in its own integrity, rather than doctoring it, and mount the discussion on more general theological or Christian principles. That is a form of faithfulness to what the text said *then*, so far as it may be discerned, but it leaves it as a museum piece, and does not attend to how the text has functioned and still functions in the churches.

The reinterpreters are in a less defensible position, if they are arguing that their version is what the Bible was saying all along, only no one noticed.

This book seeks to show that the Christian faith is intrinsically green.[78]

That claim is doubtful, as 'green' is understood today, and considering the human emphasis of the New Testament. Yet theology has stayed alive by reinterpreting (as, indeed, has biblical studies) and has gained credence by connecting the new with the old. And if the reinterpreters, like the radicals, defend their version from attitudes and beliefs gained from the Bible more generally, and particularly from an understanding of Jesus Christ, they have a kind of faithfulness, too. But no contemporary writer of ecotheology can have an uncomplicated relationship with the creation stories (including the Wisdom version) of the Old Testament.

I am, myself, greatly attracted to the radical position. There is so much that no one affirms now (except the minority of creationists with whom I am not concerned here), like the week-long creation of all species. Old dogmatic questions lose their bite in the light of modern biblical scholarship or other modern views. For instance, it has been dogmatically important to affirm that God created out of nothing, so that there is no other ultimate power in creation. But modern scholars are of the opinion that Genesis 1 suggests that God created out of the primal chaos. If that is the case, the belief in creation out of nothing has no connection with Genesis 1. So there has to be picking and choosing in use of the text, if it is used, and its interpretation. Thus feminists choose to emphasize that the image of

God in Genesis 1 is both male and female, but little use is made of Eve coming from Adam's rib.

Moreover, taking the chapter as a whole, the world described in Genesis 1 is so *tidy*, so *ordered*, with a place for everything, and everything in its place. Thus McDaniel, describing critically the 'dream' of Genesis 1, writes:

> It suggests that there was a time in the history of earth when perfect harmony obtained: when neither humans nor animals had to rob one another in order to live.[79]

Yet, as I quoted in the previous section, von Rad found dominion over animals written into the text. The harmony McDaniel describes may be found again in Psalm 104, the great psalm of nature, where human beings go to bed before lions come out. If the world were, or had ever been, like that, the ecological crisis would be more easily cured, because there would be a basic harmony to restore. But in fact that description is far from the contingent interaction of life upon accident-prone Earth. In any case, I myself have departed entirely from all description of a God who directly (or even indirectly) *causes* the natural world either instantly, through the Word, or through evolution. My conclusion is that in many ways, departing from the ancient text is the only way to address the present.

Yet the thinking of the Christian church has been channelled by these texts, and to address the *church* on present issues it is arguable that reinterpretation of the most critical parts may convey a meaning which allows people to respond as part of their Christianity. This is not a patronizing attitude of making things palatable, for any theologian will also have been shaped by these narratives, but has the duty to express the faith in present circumstances. In line with all that, I have kept the notion of the image of God, as something perceptible which, so to speak, says 'God' to us. But I have enlarged its basis to include all creation, and narrowed its occasions to times when the relationship with God, in all its human range, or its less complex non-human range, produces wonder or insight. The question now is whether something similar can be done with dominion, or whether that is a term to be departed from.

It is not hard to find relatively recent examples among both Catholics and Protestants of the unself-conscious equation of dominion with domination or mastery. That is particularly noticeable in theologies of work, for human work, with the human control that implied, was justified as the response to the divine command. That belief appears in many papal pronouncements.

> Man was created in God's image, and was commanded to conquer the earth with all it contains and to rule the world in justice and holiness; he was to acknowledge God as the maker of all things and relate himself and the totality of creation to him, so that through the dominion of all things by man the name of God would be majestic in all the earth.[80]

The viewpoint behind this is that 'man' should improve the natural world by humanizing it:

> God has confided [the earth] to his care that he may put his stamp upon it, give it a human face and figure, integrate it with his own life and so fulfil it.[81]

This is clearly the opposite of relationship. Just as God was believed to act in what is predominantly a male way by causing effects which overcame the natural, so were human beings in their sphere. But given what human beings are sometimes capable of in their conquering, the case for a shift in perception has become urgent. Yet in 1975 Don Cupitt was still urging that:

> Christians must find courage to affirm that wild nature is not enough, because it is prehuman and premoral. Through man's work wilderness is to be made a garden, the animal kingdom to come to praise its maker, and raw minerals, the products of volcanoes, earthquakes and sedimentation, to be made into great sculpture and buildings.[82]

The other theological point in these quotations is that human beings offer up the conquered world to God (as Christ puts all beneath God's feet?). The *fulfilling* of the natural world by such action echoes a belief that the non-human world receives its meaning, certainly its theological meaning, from its humanization. Once more von Rad finds this already in the Genesis text.

> Thus man's creation has a retroactive significance for all non-human creatures; it gives them a new relation to God. The creature, in addition to having been created by God, receives through man a responsibility to God; in any case, because of man's dominion it receives once again the dignity belonging to a special domain of God's sovereignty.[83]

Whether or not von Rad is right to see a retroactive significance in the text, the developed notion that the non-human world receives its significance from humans can scarcely survive the knowledge that human beings arrived in the last moments of evolutionary time, unless one is also prepared to say that the preceding aeons were empty as far as value to God is concerned. It is not surprising that the Christian faith has been called anthropocentric, far beyond inescapable human limitation and into human hubris. The belief that nature acquires its importance to God through human beings also undergirds some thoroughgoing accounts of humans as priests of creation, and more will be said of that later.

From another neck of the Christian woods comes a World Council of Churches' paper on 'God in Nature and History' published in 1968, and thus just at the beginning of Christian consciousness of the state of the natural world as a religious issue. On the one hand this paper shows sensitivity enough to call nature 'our sister', and to champion nature conservation. On the other hand, when the issue of technology is raised, nature loses that character of relationship. It has to be stripped of anything that would stand in humanity's way.

> During the last decade the conviction has often been voiced that modern technology is a fruit of the gospel, a result of man's calling to dominate the earth in the name and as the image of God . . . Man has always to some extent tried to control nature and to make tools which could help him in this struggle. Hampered, however, by his belief that nature was the external manifestation of the

Godhead, and that a deep change of its course and function might evoke the wrath of the gods, his technical skill and outreach necessarily remained very limited . . . The greatest stumbling-block for a radical display of man's dominating force was removed when, as a result of Christian preaching in the Western world, nature was understood as the creation of a transcendent God, and was thus desacralized and de-demonized.[84]

It has to be repeated that the belief was that human domination of the natural world was a good thing, and the more the better, materially and theologically. Along with that goes the belief reflected in the last sentence of the quotation, that God was to be encountered in history, not in the natural world, which was believed to give rise to idolatry. Only in a few cases was a direct relationship between God and the natural world envisaged. Against that I have emphasized the immanence of God's being-with all creation. That does not deny transcendence. God is not a domesticated local divinity whose outward manifestation is the natural world *simpliciter*, although from time to time that may image God's desires and purposes. It remains true that God exceeds every present infinitely. Yet, if God let be in freedom and accompanies creation in love, the divine presence is there in every situation, including those in which human technology is used for or against the well-being of the natural world.

Since beliefs of the kind reported here were the normal expression of Christianity in relation to the natural world until the 1970s, it is not surprising that Lynn White should have concluded in his seminal 1967 article:

We shall continue to have a worsening ecological crisis until we reject the Christian axiom that nature has no reason for existing save to serve man.[85]

By all accounts it was White's article that galvanized the churches and theology first into denial, then into a more sober evaluation and reinterpretation. His own article can certainly be criticized for sweeping historical generalizations and the overstatement of his case. There never was a time when *homo sapiens*, like other creatures, was not taking from the environment whatever was possible: it is not simply a Christian malpractice. Environmental archaeology has unearthed the same habits in 7000-year-old settlements.

> There is little to suggest that past human groups were any less exploitative of their environment – or any less spendthrift in their consumption of its resources – than we are today. The assumption that all past societies were well adapted to their environments – noble savages in the garden of Eden – owes more to late 20th-century wishful thinking than to reality. It was simply that their numbers were fewer and hence their overall impact appears less. There has never been an ecological golden age.[86]

Even given this qualifying of Lynn White's charge, however, the theological bases which led to Christian inaction in a world of growing population and increasingly powerful technology cry out for reinterpretation. I would say reinterpretation more often than a departure from the Genesis text, because the intelligence and management skills that only humanity has will be needed to approach the complex problems. For that reason stewardship will be considered in a later section. Yet more than these skills is needed; if they do not arise out of an underlying sense of relationship, nothing will have basically changed in humanity's sense of the natural world, and John Black's version of the accusation against Christianity will still have point.

> If Christianity will be shown in the end to have failed the world, it will have failed because it encouraged man to set himself apart from nature, or, at the very least, because it failed to discourage him from doing so.[87]

It can be argued, however, that this distaste for domination is effortless in a city-dweller who has never had to wrench her own living from the land. Actual experience of the contrariness of nature, or its downright malevolence (terms which personify nature, as happens in these struggles), would make it clear that nothing short of dominion, or even domination, is required. It was equally required from the beginning of farmers working the arid, stony soils of ancient Palestine.

But the matter at issue is not one of occasional anger and frustration when, for instance, the weather ruins a crop. The criticism, rather, is of the settled attitude towards the natural world in terms of a *war* which humanity must *win*. The change of outlook being recommended is one from warfare to co-operation, even though nature is not always ready to co-operate, and may arouse the picturesque language farmers are famous for.

In his book *The Control of Nature*, John McPhee scrupulously avoids value judgments, but describes graphically: the ingenious damming of a volcanic lava flow threatening an Icelandic town; the efforts of the US Corps of Engineers to direct the Mississippi along preferred channels, thus saving New Orleans and a raft of industries; the problems of maintaining homes in the San Gabriel mountains at Los Angeles, amid the frequent landslides of fault-line shattered debris.[88]

To anyone whose home and economy is not bound up in these issues it seems startling, not to say foolhardy, that people should live and work where such danger, and hence such costs and efforts, are involved. As McPhee comments on the never-ending struggle with the Mississippi: 'the nation could not afford nature'.[89] These are instances of 'boundary situations' for human life on this planet, and each may be judged differently. It is worth commenting *en route*, however, that as the world's population grows, and global warming renders more areas arid, more such boundary situations, without the money to modify them, may well be encountered. What is immediately interesting, however, is the language used in reviews on the book's cover, but not in the text: 'Three monumental acts of defiance against Mother Nature' (*The Observer*); 'Three battlefields in humanity's global war against nature' (*The New York Times*).

Whether or not it is felt to be necessary to preserve New Orleans and the industries along the present banks of the Mississippi; whether or not one may feel that the public money for ever to be spent in making the San Gabriels habitable would be better allocated to dealing with the problems which drove people there in the first place; the attitude to what is going on, and what is to be done, will be very different if the language and mind-set of 'global war' is transformed into 'global co-operation'. Various features of the natural world may sometimes show themselves unwilling and capricious companions (why, after all, should we expect them to bend to every human enterprise?), but we do share the planet with them. So it behoves us, quite apart from the theological perspective of God's presence, to get along with them.

One other illustration will make the same point. In the summer of 1995 a British woman climber died. In every single media account that I saw, heard or read, it was pointed out that she had earlier 'conquered' Everest. The view of humans and mountains revealed by the language of conquering is the same old dominating mind-set: it is as if the mountain were a slave once it had been climbed. Exactly the same language was used of Edmund Hillary's 'conquest' of Everest for the first time in 1953, so the greening of consciousness in the media, and perhaps in the public at large, is very partial.

I am told that the verb for a climb like this in the Sherpa language connotes 'making friends with the mountain', getting to know it, appreciate it, live with it. Such a concept, with its lack of dominating overtones, even on a difficult expedition, begins to show the way in which such control of nature as humanity requires in order to live may go along with appreciation of the natural 'other', so that co-operation becomes a possibility. Then religiously endorsed concepts of warfare and conquering may give way to those of interaction and concurrence with God and nature, while humanity's self-understanding becomes a little less given to self-glorification.

'Dominion', therefore, is a word so tending towards unfeeling mastery that it seems incompatible with imaging a God of freedom and love, who works by attraction rather than by force. I judge the word to be so dangerous that it is to be departed from in any contemporary doctrine of creation.

6. The moral standing of the non-human

The case against dominion as domination, and the case for a particularly sensitive form of stewardship, will be strengthened if non-human creation is acknowledged to have a moral standing. That is not to say that non-human creature may themselves be moral. Some animals may learn what is permitted and what is not, and I have known a cat look and sound (by a distinctive yowling) guilty for being in a forbidden part of the house. But, as far as we now know, only human reflective self-consciousness has gone beyond an appearance of morality in learned behaviour.

What is being proposed instead is that non-human creatures have moral *standing*, so that their lives merit human moral consideration, and hence also consideration in such practical matters as decisions on land use. In other words, non-human life has to be shown to have value, which may be the instrumental value of usefulness, or the more critical intrinsic value, which holds that it is good that such beings should be, whether or not they are useful or beautiful to human valuers.

In one sense Christian theology may have a short answer to all that when it is believed that God values all creatures. All creatures thus have value to a valuer, and intrinsic value at that, since they are valued for what they are. There may be a sense in which all creatures, including human beings , also have instrumental value to God as well, providing God with experiences not otherwise procurable by bringing about instances of finite freedom with love or an appetite for life. All mutual relationship presumes that virtuous kind of instrumental value in its give and take. But what is being derived from such relationship is very different from the kind of instrumental valuing which regards the other only as a useful commodity.

The belief that God values all creatures might well be sufficient to impel Christians into action. But it would be a very hollow kind of action if the agents themselves had no such values, so that obedience to God's peculiar preferences for the flourishing of non-human nature became the only motive. In the end, therefore, although Christianity has an extra dimension in environmental ethics, since

God let be the world which creatures then made, and accompanies their lives in love, the case for *human* valuation of the natural world still has to be made. Without that conviction no triple synergy, the working together of divine, natural and human energies, is possible.

A beginning to this valuation of the natural world is made even when it is seen primarily in terms of resources for human use. A resource, in order to remain a resource, has to be *sustained*. That carefulness, which measures the world's contents in terms of finite, often non-renewable, resources, could supersede the free-for-all (a very misleading term) of 'there's plenty more where that came from' which, in its myopic demand for present gratification, is still around. Thus the World Commission on Environment and Development writes:

> If needs are to be met on a sustainable basis the Earth's natural resource base must be conserved and enhanced. Major changes in policies will be needed to cope with the industrial world's current high levels of consumption, the increases in consumption needed to meet minimum standards in developing countries, and expected population growth. However, the case for the conservation of nature should not rest only with development goals. It is part of our moral obligation to other living beings and future generations.[90]

The usefulness perceived in resources may be for the present, or may be husbanded for future generations. It may consist of genetic material, minerals, places of recreation or ecotourist attraction, or the aesthetic appreciation of diversity or beauty. The result in all cases is more careful use, and it may lead to the beginnings of a more 'biocentric' view of the world. Thus the mountain gorillas of Zaire, for instance, may be preserved as much because there are rich (in local terms) tourists willing to pay to come to see them as because they and their environment are respected by local people (who may indeed be hungry for land: a human problem which also needs to be addressed). In sheerly practical terms, in the matter of bringing about conservation, an appeal to some form of self-interest in preservation may move bureaucratic or political mountains which no amount of high-souled recommendation could budge.

Such programmes as preserving rain-forests for their potential future use in medicine, however, remain thoroughly human-centred instrumental behaviour. They would require no shift of viewpoint from the WCC and papal quotations concerning the humanizing of wild nature as humanity's special task. Indeed they cohere with the traditional view expressed neatly by Calvin, that God has provided all the 'conveniences and necessaries' for human use.[91] Instrumental value of that kind on its own is inadequate for a theology, since it denies relationship, regarding the natural other as simply a commodity-in-waiting.

The very word 'resource' shows that on this basis humans remain the only important subject, since the resources are for them. But at the opposite end of the present spectrum they hold a much less prominent place in the 'deep ecology' of Aldo Leopold or of Arne Naess, which both urge a 'biocentric equality' within which all final self-realization is to be merged.[92] The extent to which this movement appears to play down the specialness of humanity disturbs some theologians.[93] Yet to some extent it begins to show what would be involved in working out the belief that God cares for *all* creatures, although God may be said to appreciate the differences among creatures as well. This is 'living as if Nature mattered', and some of its principles would carry into a Christian lifestyle that held that belief.

1. The well-being and flourishing of human and non-human life on Earth have value in themselves . . . these values are independent of the usefulness of the non-human world for human purposes.

2. Richness and diversity of life-forms contribute to the realization of these values and are also values in themselves.

3. Human beings have no right to reduce this richness and diversity except to satisfy *vital* needs.[94]

These are high ideals, underpinned in the case of many deep ecologists by a kind of earth mysticism, but their adherents are often criticized for not showing how such ideals may be implemented in practice.

> But these fine ideals often remain vague slogans without substance in the writing of deep ecology. In practice political change seems to be reduced to vague and pious calls to develop 'maturity', 'character' and 'leadership', and to go beyond the narrow ego to develop an 'ecological self' which affirms the integrity of nature in the widest sense.[95]

It is all too easy for a doctrine (religious or secular) which aims at changing perceptions to seem 'vague and pious'. Yet Marshall in this last quotation has a point, because change sooner or later involves action as well as perception. The rapid move in some deep ecologists to a mystic whole of biocentric equality will not do either for this doctrine of creation. Individuals, human and non-human, continue to matter as individuals with whom God has relationship, as well as being part of greater wholes all the way up to the planet. Without concern for individuals, concern for the whole could become undemanding wishful thinking. I have already argued that God companions every individual great tit, for instance, in its particular circumstances. Of course great tits live in an ecological system, which in the end is part of the totality of Earth, but care for the bird in one context does not remove the need for care in another. Some of the problems of environmental action, in fact, come from the difficulties of doing the best in all these contexts in which creatures live simultaneously.

It would seem, indeed, that to affirm intrinsic worth *alone* (it is good that such things as great tits should be) may in the end come to be a very conservative position in which virtually whatever is, is right. It does not help in making the priorities that are required in action on, for instance, whether fresh land should be brought under cultivation. Nor does it assist in the *inequalities* that exist across the planet, particularly the human one of the disparity between the rich North and the poor South with the consequent demands each make on the land. Further, the mystical oneness which deep ecology can evoke suggests a collapsing together of all participants into a single biosphere which becomes the all-important focus. In that picture unity becomes more important than the sets of relationships which go to make it up. Relationship, on the other hand, involves togetherness but also distinctiveness, and that requires the close distance implied by 'with' between humans and non-humans, as there is between all creation and God. That in turn, as I argued earlier, presupposes a non-invasive, non-violent form of instrumentalism. Good relationships will often include moments of union, but they are also good through recognizing the otherness of the other.

The same removal from the structure of relationship as may sometimes occur in deep ecology arises also in the question of 'rights', especially the rights of the non-human. The language of human rights has the virtue of being universally understood (if not universally practised), and it draws attention to the oppressed and the victims of human behaviour. Such rights appear as *claims* made by some, for others to recognize the *power* and *liberty* of their possessor to act within them without *obstruction*.[96] Talk of human rights has a justifiable general use as expressing strong and widely-held beliefs that there are some things human beings *cannot* do to others.

Rights language, however, again offers an ideal the practice of which is much more difficult. Agreement on a list of rights is not easily come by, and the question whether rights are political or moral is not easily solved. Do they include, for instance, Locke's insistence on the rights of property-owners? How, in practice, are the rights of property-owners balanced against the rights of the homeless?

> In practice the UN declarations of rights leave only one right unqualified – the right not to be tortured. All other rights are qualified and made subject to the needs of states.[97]

Difficulty in practice, however, would not be sufficient reason for refraining from invoking non-human (e.g. animal) rights. Many good ideals are hard to implement, and ecological questions may be extremely complex whatever ethical views are held. But the difficulty in application derives from another defect in rights models. Because rights belong to each individual, they appear to guarantee a 'territory' for that individual which may be defended against others as a kind of possession. There is a sense in which they add to ownership rather than working towards relationship. I therefore find myself in agreement with Marshall when he writes:

> In the long run, human and animal liberation do not require a charter of rights but a thorough transformation of our unjust and unequal relationships, and the development of an ecological sensibility which recognizes the intrinsic worth and autonomy of all creatures.[98]

This sense of thinking in a different framework, where quality of relationship is more important than a list of rights to life and its conditions, since life is not lived by aggregates of individuals, holds even against the most sensitive rendering of non-human rights in a framework of justice propounded by James Nash in *Loving Nature*.[99] He recognizes the problems in using this language: extending the notion of right all the way to micro-organisms may trivialize the notion; the assertion of all these rights could lead to absurdities in practice; determining and balancing rights will be endlessly complicated; respect for the rights of non-humans is hopelessly impractical. Nevertheless he champions this way of affirming the value and sacredness of all life as worthy of moral consideration.

> Advocacy for the rights of nature is the contention that environmental concern is not only an expression of benevolence, but also an obligation to justice – not simply justice to human interests, but also justice to the interests of other creatures. In Western cultures rights are important; no rights suggests no moral consideration.[100]

That last point could be strategically important, but only if a claim of rights alone is held to express moral considerability. Nash proceeds to propound a 'Bill of Biotic Rights', which shows what would have to be defended in practice as far as wild nature is concerned.

1. The right to participate in the natural competition for existence.

2. The right to satisfaction of their basic needs and the opportunity to perform their individual and/or ecosystemic functions.

3. The right to healthy or whole habitats.

4. The right to reproduce their own kind.

5. The right to fulfil their evolutionary potential with freedom from human-induced extinctions.

6. The right to freedom from human cruelty, flagrant abuse, or frivolous use.

7. The right to redress through human interventions, to restore a semblance of the natural conditons disrupted by human actions.

8. The right to a fair share of the goods necessary for the sustainability of one's species.[101]

Nash allows that these are *prima facie* rights without the universality of absolute rights, but he argues that only if there are stronger reasons for not honouring them should they be infringed. They must be relative rights, for, as Nash points out, if non-humans had absolute rights, humans would not survive. There is no doubt that Nash's list of biotic rights is both thoughtful and comprehensive. Both the evolutionary character and the present well-being of all wild creatures is comprehended. If there are political groups which recognize only the claims of rights, this would be a good list to recommend to them.

What I miss from the whole discussion in this section of his book, however, is warmth. Human relations with non-human nature become another duty rather than a way of living which emerges from renewed vision of the interrelatedness of all things. The difference may be drawn out by comparing what Nash says on responsibilities with H. R. Niebuhr's account of the responsible self.[102] Nash argues that the sense of responsibility arises out of a sense of justice and the rights that entails.

Rights provide an objective moral reference for responsibilities, because we cannot define our duties except in reference to what others are due. Responsibilities to others, in fact, *are* respect for their rights.[103]

For Niebuhr, on the other hand, responsibilities have more to do with response and responsiveness, which is considerably more than mere reaction.

What is implied in the idea of responsibility is the image of man the answerer, man engaged in dialogue, man acting in response to action upon him.[104]

This dialogue continues, and the answerer is accountable to the other for the quality of response. Thus a morality of responsibility takes place within a continuing relationship which Niebuhr expresses as dialogue. Further, whereas teleology seeks the *goal* of good action (like the consequentialist ethics to which I shall come shortly), and deontology seeks *law* to prescribe what is right (as Nash and others invoking rights do), an ethic of responsibility asks first 'What is going on?' and then seeks to make a *fitting* response to the present circumstances.

The fitting action, the one that fits into a total interaction as response and as anticipation of further response, is alone conducive to the good, and alone is right.[105]

This view of moral responsibility may seem startlingly *ad hoc*, and certainly asks a good deal of the responsible self, yet it fits with a sense of life as dynamic, open, interactive, creative and free, without denying human limitation, relation to others and accountability.

Part of our humanity is to be creatively involved in our responses to things around us, to seek to bring into being a good that does not exist in actuality. Such freedom and creativity, however, are not boundless; they are set within patterns of human relationships.[106]

As the end of that quotation shows, the discussion of responsibility as responsiveness in the 1960s concerned primarily human relationships. Niebuhr does, however, discuss the natural world, although consciousness of ecological issues was not critical then. He points out, quite correctly, that human apprehension of the natural world is largely determined by one's society. Nature has been interpreted to us, with 'a *system* of nature as *systematized* by society'.[107]

> The picture of the radical doubter who sits down before natural events like a little child to be freshly taught by them could be painted only by a generation which had made no study of little children, had paid little attention to the way in which language transmits interpretations, and knew nothing of the social, historical character of our knowledge of nature in general, of our art and our science in particular.[108]

Earlier I argued a similar case for an irreducible minimum of anthropocentricity in all human approach to the natural world. Niebuhr, however, gives that perception a gentler twist by writing of a self which is neither wholly dependent nor independent, neither fresh to nature nor totally determined by society, but which is always social, always in dialogue with its companions.

> The self before nature remains a social self, responding to other selves in all responses to nature.[109]

Patterns of relationship with the natural world, then, elicit the same kind of responsibility. First comes the question 'What is going on?' with all the information that can be gathered. Then one arrives at a fitting response, which will allow for further response in the continuing dialogue. A rudimentary instance may make this all clearer. The herds of deer in the Scottish highlands have been growing in numbers, and the effect of their grazing has become serious. From Nash's biotic rights standpoint deer and plants alike have 'the right to participate in the natural competition for existence'. In that competition the deer will always win until they run short of grazing. What Nash's scheme requires next is that the rights of every wild animal, grass, heather and so forth involved, let alone the rights of land- and herd-owners would have to be studied *individually*. Yet it is the nature of the *interaction* which is causing the difficulty.

On the other hand, if the first question of an ethic of responsibility is 'What is going on?', it is precisely the *interaction* of creatures which gives the answer. The next part of the dialogue is the arrival at a fitting human response, which in some cases may well be culling the herds for their own, as well as the general, good. The size and nature of the cull would be the next stage. That infringes no human or non-human rights, and although death ends the relationship with some individuals who are yet God's creatures, and hence at the least should have a quick and painless dispatch, it may be more fitting that that should happen than that the land should become degraded. Human beings remain accountable for their response and the dialogue goes on.

This ethical framework of relationship-within-which-there-is-a dialogue-of-responsiveness-and-responsibility takes Christian environmental ethics beyond consequentialism as well. In that ethical view one should do always what has the best consequences: in utilitarian terms these consequences are the greatest increase of pleasure over pain, or, in more recent formulations, well-being over suffering. It was the utilitarian philosopher Peter Singer who in his *Animal Liberation* (1975) alerted the world to the pain which human beings inflicted on animals, and called this speciesism, an attitude as objectionable as racism or sexism.[110]

Including animals in the calculation of well-being, with their suffering counted equally, as far as such comparisons may be made, led to a recognition that animals have *interests* in such things as food supply, habitat preservation, conditions for mating and rearing offspring, which are all part of their well-being. Scientists, with their strictly unromantic, uninvolved stance, had tended to record the natural world in terms of *mechanisms*,[111] so it was left to a philosopher in Bentham's tradition to enlarge the moral picture (and, in relation to scientists, to describe experiments using animals, criticizing the view that animals were merely 'tools for research', especially in the US with its minimal restrictions).

Singer wrote of animals as sentient beings with interests that make them morally considerable. Other writers have extended that analysis to include insects and plants. Such creatures may not raise moral issues about factory farming or scientific experimentation, and they lack the central nervous system which is our and all animals' avenue of pain, but they certainly have interests and varying degrees of flourishing.

> Plants and insects have a well-being, and they respond with a (non-felt) interest in this well-being, as when a tree sends roots down deeper for water, or . . . *Escheria coli*, a common bacterium . . . prefers glucose over lactose and eats this latter only after the former is gone.[112]

In this quotation Rolston is not arguing that these are conscious or intended preferences. Rather, this is the way in which genetic preferences work. He is not attributing subjectivity in these cases (although I wonder whether that says more about our incapacity to measure subjectivity in, for instance, trees). What Rolston argues is that even where there is no subjectivity, life remains. His description is a commentary on the category of appreciation of life, which is the basis of the relationship with God.

> There is an object-with-will, even though there is no subject-with-will. The organism is genetically programmed to argue, to probe, to fight, to run, to grow, to reproduce, to resist death.[113]

Rolston is arguing for finding value already present in the natural world rather than calculating its future well-being. He can likewise advance his consideration from individual non-human creatures to include the ecosystem in which they live.

> Ecosystems are not as coherent as organisms, but are not randomly fortuitous either; they fit together with a characteristically systems structure. Situated environmental fitness for organisms often yields a complicated life together.[114]

'Situated environmental fitness' may perhaps be taken as more than a description. If it became a value to humans, referring not only to non-human creatures but to themselves, in the way that at present their own intelligence or complexity is a value, the problems of excess and callousness would be seen to be inhuman. I shall take that further later. To return to Rolston, however, he praises the unintentionally creative *process* of ecological systems whose whole is greater in 'richness, beauty, integrity and dynamic stability' than any of its component parts. It represents 'intrinsic values woven into instrumental relationships', which may certainly be affirmed in addition to the importance of the individual.

There is no doubt that Christianity may learn a lot from this enlightened view of non-human well-being. In one sense, certainly, the increase in moral standing of so many creatures simply multiplies problems in ethical practice, as well as requiring the kind of redirected doctrine of creation I am proposing here. That multi-plication of problems is particularly the case with utilitarianism which, like rights ethics, dwells on the individual, so that the calculating of consequences to the well-being of all involved one by one becomes extremely daunting. There are also questions about the well-being of what harms humanity, for instance the HIV virus, to which I shall return. In any case the Christian slant on well-being, which I shall come to shortly, is involved less in calculating the greatest amount of well-being than in a relationship to those involved in a particular situation – although that version, too, admittedly has its own difficulties.

One virtue, however, of thinking in terms of relationship rather than in rights or consequences is that *a priori* hierarchical notions of place in a graded moral community do not appear and have to be justified. But it is worthwhile to consider the problems which various types of hierarchy within a delimited community produce. One instance of the bottom of such a hierarchy comes when Singer, concerned with animals, has notions of moral duty coming to an end at around the level of the shrimp. For Rolston, every creature making for negentropy, that is, working against the dissipation of energy in the world, is morally considerable as it clings to life and resists death. Nash comes to much the same conclusion:

Perhaps the line can be drawn at least at the juncture, in so far as identifiable, where life is distinguished from non-life, since non-living elements – like rocks and gases – have no apparent interests or drives to survive about which rights can be [meaningfully predicated].[115]

Nash is right to be cautious about the boundary to life. The HIV virus, for instance, is a complex chemical compound which *comes alive* in a host.

It has no survival instinct, no direction, no life, except what we offer it.[116]

Nash is also careful to find value in, if not rights for, 'abiotic elements', since the weather, and inanimate parts of its habitat, may contribute to the creature's well-being. His hierarchy, therefore, does not cover everything that has to be considered.

Thus the bottom end of a hierarchical moral community is somewhat obscure. The middle reaches are most clearly delineated by process theologians who assign increasing importance to 'richness of experience', so that a kingfisher, for instance, which has a wider range of experience than an amoeba, is morally more significant. Thus Charles Birch writes:

Why rate all life of equal value? If intrinsic value is measured by richness of experience, it follows that creatures such as primates and whales have more intrinsic value than worms and mosquitoes. There is a scale of intrinsic value which presumably bears some relation to the development of the nervous system of the organism. I would have no difficulty in applauding the campaign of the World Wildlife Fund to save the chimpanzees of Africa. Nor have I any difficulty in applauding the campaign of the World Health Organization to eradicate the smallpox virus and the malarial parasite.[117]

That certainly appears to settle the discussion. The greater the sentience, the more effort humans should put into letting such richness of experience be. Where there is little of such richness, no tears should be shed over human-directed extinction. Nash supports this grading, although he is sensitive to the 'hierarchicalism' implicit in it 'that has been the source of multiple forms of human oppression, including racism and sexism, as well as domination over nature'.[118]

Exactly! Why this grading should escape such undesirable consequences when others did not is not made clear. Thus I cannot agree with Nash when he advocates equality in human *intra*-species rights, but a degree of inequality in *inter*-species rights, which does not prevent, although it is supposed to restrict, humans from destroying members of other species. Nash concludes:

> Graded rankings seem indispensable – even inevitable – in making ethical judgments in conflict situations involving humans and other life forms.[119]

Human beings after all, swat flies to prevent them landing on their food without giving the matter any moral thought. Only at the end of his discussion does Nash revert to interdependence among creatures. Graded rankings, he holds, 'occur in the context of, and with respect for, relationality'.

But what kind of relationship could exist alongside behaviour so implicitly judgmental as to assign *a priori* degrees of intrinsic value? In the kind of responsive relationship I have been deriving from Niebuhr the first question is 'What is happening here?', not 'What degrees of intrinsic value are represented in these individuals?'. The happening and the interaction have prime initial importance. But for the process writers Daly and Cobb such importance is not to be confused with intrinsic value.

> The judgment of intrinsic value is quite different from the judgment of importance of a species to the interrelated whole. The interrelated whole would probably survive the extinction of chimpanzees with little damage, but it would be seriously disturbed by the extinction of some species of bacteria.[120]

The authors are opposing a different grading here – one geared to value only if the organism contributes to the survival of the planet. It may indeed be agreed that creatures may be valuable even if they do not contribute to such survival. Yet this opposition of one grading of values against another raises questions about ranked intrinsic value in practice. If bacteria with their minimal richness of experience have little intrinsic value, on Daly and Cobb's scale, they will 'deserve' only tardy ethical consideration, by which time the effect of their loss on 'the interrelated whole' may be devastating.

In present circumstances plankton has this basic importance. The richness of experience of plankton may well be less than that of all who feed on them. But the deleterious effect of global warming on their marine habitat becomes a serious issue because plankton is at the beginning of important food chains. The whole notion of richness of experience as the basis of a gradation in intrinsic value comes from a reading of evolution as an upward progress in complexity, and it is virtually unusable as a criterion in face of the complicated atmospheric and inter-species problems in the ecological crisis.

If the vertical ranking of species has its problems, what would a horizontal biological egalitarian propose? Nash finds egalitarianism implicitly misanthropic because he understands it to mean that humans are lumped together with other forms.

> Biotic egalitarianism places all species – dandelions and dogs, humans and amoebas, or, in restricted forms, all of a class of species like mammals, from mice to humans – on the same moral plane.[121]

But Stephen Clark, who embraces this way of thinking, points out that *human* egalitarianism does not entail indifference to the particularities of people, nor, as many fear, a simple diffusion of resources equally to all. Instead, the aim is to ensure that no class of person has such advantages as to make life not worth living for others.

> We seek to ensure that every person (or rather, realistically, every fellow citizen) has a roughly similar chance to live a life of her choosing, in company with others having a like chance . . . The same system can be imagined for wider egalitarians: we should

seek to act according to rules that allow all sorts of creatures a fair chance of living a life of their choosing . . .[122]

Clark is certainly a more considered and less potentially misanthropic egalitarian than some other writers, but this quotation shows a basic fairness which could only be denied if it is axiomatic that humanity may always behave in ways which deny other creatures the possibility of 'living a life of their choosing'.

The very notion that intrinsic value can come in degrees is dubious. The attribution functions more as a declaration of status – this is a being with independent worth – than an ontological characteristic of which one may have more or less. Moreover, for such value to be graded it has to be measured against some standard for comparison. The 'richness of experience' criterion points to that standard being humanity. Cobb's 1972 description of 'a healthy biotic pyramid with man at its apex' is still (so to speak) the bottom line.[123]

But to recognize that human beings have capacities which other creatures do not is one thing; to measure the value of the being of the rest in relation to the absolute (or working absolute) of human value is to be blind from the beginning to the otherness of other creatures, both as themselves and in their 'situated environmental fitness', as Rolston neatly called it. It would doom any form of relation other than top-down paternalism. In the end it becomes the criterion: 'the more creatures are like me, the more I should do for them', all of which is another form of praise to humanity by humanity.

The problems of all versions of graded rankings come to a head, in all senses, with humanity at the top. Certainly human beings are the only moral agents, and in that, as in other ways, they differ from all other creatures. But the ecological crisis has come about because human beings saw no relationship between themselves and the rest of creation, so an ethic based on human superiority, no matter how much the rest of creation is found to be 'good for themselves' (Nash), will not do.[124]

Thus far this section has been rather like a tour on an open-topped double-decker bus, of the kind many cities in Britain are familiar with. The 'sights' (rights, consequences, hierarchies of value) have been pointed out *en route* as the bus moves on. It is time now to leave the bus, indeed leave the metaphor, and describe what a Christian environmental ethic of responsiveness and response might be.

Christian ethics for human morality among *human beings* has regularly been shaped by the understood form and content of the divine relationship with human beings. But there has been so little in the theological tradition about God's relationship with the *natural* world, as opposed to God's *provision* of nature as a set of resources for human beings, that no such starting point of divine-nature relations for human morality among non-human beings has been possible. But if theology is triadic rather than dyadic, that is, it is about the flow of relationships among God, human beings and the natural world, the situation is different, for there now exists a pattern of divine-nature relations to guide action.

The relationships, as I have said frequently, are mutual but not symmetrical, since fundamentally what is offered in a relationship is one's *being*. Being, as being, is what has intrinsic value: the precious marvel that anything has become possible, and *is*. Offered in relationship, that intrinsic value is allowed to become available for the enjoyment, well-being and benefit of others. The divine being is offered freely to all in the form of love – as the Logos of divine being is enacted in Jesus Christ. Non-human being is what it is as a lichen, a tree frog or a great white shark. With whatever capacities, beauty or situated environmental fitness it has within its ecosystem, each creature is an instance of intrinsic value continually in relation with, and hence of virtuous instrumental value to, other non-human beings.

The individual and the interaction are offered to God as a response to the divine gift of possibility, and to human beings as an enlargement of their life made possible by fellow creatures. (I cannot know that such responses are made with whatever degree of consciousness a non-human creature may have; but this is the role all such creatures play in the triple relationship as discerned by a human being.) Human beings have a far greater range of possibility than non-human beings, with their social, moral, aesthetic and intellectual capacities. But it is again their *being*, with these capacities, which is offered to God in relation, and to the best possible well-being of their fellow creatures, human and non-human, in a continuing relationship in which human responsiveness and responsibility is exercised in its present range of possibility.

That is the fundamental theological picture out of which actual ethical practice towards the natural world arises. It is a picture to which all notions of 'rights' are irrelevant and would be fatal if introduced. Rights are precisely what one must insist on when there is *no* relationship, or only one of top-down domination. The concept may be useful in the present political world to give easily recognized expression to a minimum standard of life, but it has no place in a theological picture which is all about relationships. That does not mean to say that such a useful formulation as Nash's 'biotic rights' is irrelevant in Christian environmental thought, but they function as *principles* guiding behaviour in a relationship rather than as rights which imply no relationship and may be demanded as a moral commodity.[125]

Consideration of consequences remains important in a relationship, and much human action in the natural world, as in its human counterpart, will be guided by probable outcomes. The greatest possible flourishing of the natural world remains an aim, as in utilitarianism. But it is an aim occurring in sets of relationships, which at the very least changes the tone and the ultimate target. The flourishing of the natural world enables its continuing response to *God* as well as to humans; human work for that flourishing turns the possibility of possibilities into particular possibilities in nature for the free exercise of appetite for life, and so responds to *God* through action in the natural world. There may, in that process, be a human working teleology which is directed towards ends in the future rather than now! But it is in the present moment of action on the human side, and flourishing on the non-human side that the divine purposes for the world are achieved.

But what about the problems every environmental ethic has to face? It is simply not possible for all of creation to flourish simultaneously and together. But a distinction has to be made here.

Some aspects of the natural world, such as food chains, do not pose moral issues of the kind human beings face. These practices, however much human beings may regret them, represent the way life has developed and made its own world with its own freedom. The real problems for human beings come in conflict situations, when they have to exercise management in such matters as protecting species, regulating industry, or practising agriculture. Would a graded set of priorities not be required in these cases? I believe not, or at least not in the shape of a firmly based *a priori* gradation, although priorities undoubtedly have to be arrived at.

Here Niebuhr's proposal of a well-informed (What is going on?) fitting response within a dialogue gives direction, if not easy answers. Before coming to the point of answers, however, it is well to remember that Niebuhr recognized that all human responses to nature are social interpretations, not simple, natural truth. Information-gathering in that case includes being alive to the differences of human view and hence interpretation between, say, industry, a government tourist board and a 'green' non-governmental organization. Being the people we are, we are likely to exercise the 'hermeneutics of suspicion' more on the statements of those groups with whom we have less sympathy. But if self-consciousness is the vaunted characteristic of humanity, making us different from the other creatures, we may at least be aware of the pitfalls in the interpretative process.

Being well informed includes knowing who and what are involved, how they interact, what the probable outcomes of various actions might be, and so forth. That is rarely easy, and the real point against the prior gradation is that each set of circumstances is different, and that the information required and the fitting response (one which fits that particular situation) will be equally varied, while the dialogue goes on and is never finally settled.

In all that variation there can be no guarantee that humanity will always merit greater consideration. The facile hypothetical question 'In a fire would you rescue your grandmother or your cat?' does not even begin to approach the real problems of the world. Should an industry be given a greenfield site? Should a convenient road run through a site of particular beauty or scientific interest? Should a country in debt to the First World be encouraged to give its best land to the intensive farming of cash crops? It is far from clear that the well-informed fitting response in these situations will be in favour of human projects.

But I am not offering answers to such problems here because the whole tenor of responsiveness within a relationship is that answers depend on the particular circumstances. A self-aware and defended use of principles, however, keeps such practice from being too spasmodically *ad hoc* in arriving at the response. Nash's 'biotic rights' used as principles to guide decision would be useful even in the particularities of any individual case. He advocates for non-human creatures, for instance, 'freedom from human cruelty, flagrant abuse or frivolous use', which may well serve as a criterion for judgment. In the end, however, Clark's conclusion holds:

> Much of this must be left to concrete occasions and to careful agents, rather than being settled with a flourish of high principles.[126]

The other point to be gained from Niebuhr is that the response is not the end of the story. It fits into a dialogue. Thus the ecological crisis is not a series of discrete probelms to be solved one by one scientifically, although such scientific input is vital. One of the first books, in fact, to alert the public to environmental dangers was Rachel Carson's *Silent Spring* of 1962, which showed the inadequacies of piecemeal problem-solving by demonstrating the knock-on effects of the use of pesticides.[127] The state of the natural world, and of human beings, and of the interaction between them as the result of our action, is the ground for the next part of the dialogue, and we are partly accountable through our decisions or equally by our inaction for that state. Such dialogue-in-relationship is endlessly difficult as well as immensely rewarding. But above all it is part of our response in freedom and love to God.

One last facet remains to be considered in this general overview of the framework within which non-human nature has moral standing. If the aim is the flourishing of the natural world's response to God, can such flourishing ever be contemplated for the HIV virus, which may stand here for all parts of the natural world noxious to human beings? It is indeed probable that some writers propose the grading of value and assignment of rights in some forms of ethics as a means to exclude such creatures from the moral community.

Yet the HIV virus is as much a response to possibility as a golden eagle, although a much simpler one that happens to cause direct damage to human beings. It is not the only immunodeficiency virus, as if human beings were particularly singled out. There are others in cats, cattle and five species of monkeys. They all occur naturally and spread when conditions are right. If the ethical emphasis is on a definable moral *community*, then the exclusion of these viruses is understandable. But that does raise questions about the viruses' relation to God. Has the virus no relation to God, so that human beings may exclude it from their care? Are there creatures that by their very nature are morally negative? That would seem to set up another form of dualism.

If, however, one works less with the notion of a moral community which has fixed borders, and more with several sets of *relationships* among which the fitting response has to be made, then there need be no dualism. The immunodeficiency viruses are accepted as natural, as occurring within the presence of God, just as the diseases they enable occur within the presence of God, as do the sufferers' lives. The fitting response is overwhelmingly likely to be the seeking of a cure for the disease, but not because the virus is in any moral sense 'evil', a term which would mystify, indeed demonize it, but because in the ongoing balance of human responsibility in relation to God and to the other inhabitants of Earth this is the most fitting thing to do in these circumstances.

When relationships rather than community form the moral basis, then nothing is *a priori* excluded. Not only disease-bearing creatures, but also the most minute of micro-organisms, the geological components of a habitat, the minerals which are so often the object of human covetousness, climates with their possible changes, and indeed everything that is possible in and around the Earth are included. Relationship may even be expressed in non-intervention, as when a wilderness is left to be itself. God, after all, in the first place, let be. In all of this, human accountability is so great that it is as well that there is joy and companionship in relationship with fellow creatures, human and non-human, as well as concern for their well-being.

7. Models of relationship

Although relationships, as simply expressing a connection, may be of all kinds, I have used the word in this book with positive and enlarging connotations. I have argued that the answer to 'What does God do?' is not a series of powerful, virile interventions, but the steady, faithful maintaining of relationships with all that is and has ever been. Such action of God's may only be recognized by human beings (and we would have no means of knowing if it were recognized elsewhere), but a God of love would not exclude anything from relationship that had made use of possibility to *be*. God has always been believed to know, with a totality of understanding, humanity in general, humans in particular groupings, and individual women and men.

> Thou knowest my downsitting and mine uprising, thou understandest my thought afar off (Ps.139.2, AV).

If no creature is excluded from the divine companionship, however, the same kind of totality of divine knowledge must be involved for each one. And the loving concern which is also attributed to God will again be involved over each creature's possibilities of life. What, then, would God know and care about, say, a cheetah? Presumably God would know the whole evolutionary history of cheetahs, and the history of this particular cheetah; the cheetah's physical components of particles and molecules; its biological nature as a carnivore and its relation to other big cats; the ecological niche it occupies in the local system; its success or failure in finding food supply, in mating, and in its rearing of cubs (at least if it is a female cheetah). Such knowledge would concern both cheetahs generally and the specific happenings of this particular cheetah's life. God knows how the world looks and smells to a cheetah. Equally the divine presence will see the grace and power of the cheetah at full stretch after prey; will know its frustration at failure and its satisfaction at a successful kill which it can keep from hyenas and other predators.

God will know that cheetahs have specialized in speed, and have thereby narrowed their chances of survival, which are always greatest for a generalist. Their speed in the chase is not matched by strength in defending a kill. (When I heard this calmly described, on television as ever, I was so sorry that something as beautiful as a running cheetah could, in that very beauty, damage its own chances. Where Isaiah pictured lions lying down with lambs, perhaps one could dream of cheetahs running *with* antelopes, even with hyenas! It is not out of keeping with belief in a God of love to believe that God, too, regrets the outcome of this splendid specialization.) But God will also know the antelope's experience of the cheetah as predator; the local human beings' view of it, as predator and as a creature with symbolic power; the white hunter's view of it as quarry, with all the hinterland of beliefs and practices which that implies.

This is as far as I can go in even imagining what God might know and might feel (no love without feeling) in relation to this particular cheetah. Of course I am describing human knowledge in as rounded a form as I may, for as a human being of my time I cannot do anything else, and ascribing that, at least, to God. The point is that all that happens inside, outside and around the cheetah, and all that affects it from afar, has the ultimate significance of occurring within its relationship with God. Anything that happens to the cheetah, then, whether naturally or through human action, happens within that relationship. From that instance of the cheetah one must extrapolate to all creatures great and small, wild and tame, past, present and future. Yet God's love, like God's presence, is not made thin and general by being offered to all. The divine presence and love is constant and does not admit of degrees, so they are concentrated on each individual at each time, and are as total for non-human beings as for human beings.

I do not believe that God foreknows all that is going to happen and be done. Even foreknowledge as opposed to foreordination cannot escape the charge of determinism, with no real freedom on the part of creation. And in all this shifting, changing, problematic world, how is a God who foreknows the outcome to companion those wrestling with the interacting, indeterminate possibilities of the ecological crisis? The process theology account of God's knowledge carries more conviction with me: that God knows the actual as actual and the possible as possible – with a completeness, of course, far outstripping any little local human, but with no assured certainty of the outcome.[128] God in relation, thus, is *in* the process, *with* the creatures, not *over* or *beyond* the interrelated processes of the world.

In all of this companionship God does not interfere with the freedom of the creatures. God does not hide the antelope from the cheetah, or keep the hyenas occupied while a hungry cheetah family feeds. These are lives that creatures have made out of possibility and, in its better and worse, this is where freedom has taken creation. But in this matter of involvement humans do not stand to other creatures as God does. We are fellow-creatures, part of the hurly-burly; we affect other creatures whatever we do. The theological point in that case is that if God is believed to desire the good of creatures; if, then, their free use of possibility and appetite for life matter; then the extended range of human capacity in relation to God has among its responsibilities (its fitting response to its Creator) the cultivation and enabling of such life. How, in general, this may be done is best approached through consideration of models of relationship.

Companionship. The first and most important relation, the one on which all others are based and from which they take their character, is that of companion. If human beings cannot see themselves as sharing this planet (as companions, literally, share bread) with the rest of creation, then all the features of the ecological crisis, from overpopulation to pollution, will simply spiral on to catastrophe – catastrophe for human beings, among others.

George Hendry once complained that in traditional Christian theology 'creation is merged with providence and virtually disappears behind it'.[129] Many possible roles for human beings in relation to nature do indeed reflect its providential (useful) aspect. But companionship is about creation as creation, creatures together (being-with), sharing a history, a planet and a relationship with God. Companions are more than those who happen to be thrown together. Among human beings there is the warmth of fellowship in the relation, and one is *drawn* by attraction, not forced, commanded or landed into the relationship. There are, naturally, differences in the reciprocity human companionship can expect from the natural world, yet, like the all-human version, this is not a duty which one had better perform. If there is no warmth of feeling about nature, no enjoyment of its very being and pleasure in its company, there will be no companionship. And if there is no companionship, the other forms of relationship will be entirely duty, the exercise of the Christian superego, admirable in its way, but fundamentally lacking in love.

Companions remain themselves while simultaneously being bound together in relationship. Thus companionship 'can express natural and human interdependence without excluding the distinctiveness of each, for companions are involved together in what they may be doing, yet retain their own identities in the process'.[130] Thus both dependence and independence occur in a healthy companionship. Humanity is dependent on the proper functioning of all the natural support systems of the planet (air, water, food), but is also a unique species with its own range of capacity. Conversely, the natural world has its own independent varied and intrisically valuable character, which no *companion* would wantonly damage, but it is also dependent on the powerful human species refraining from overwhelming invasion and exploitation, and instead working for its well-being.

Some kinds of action become impossible when companionship is taken seriously. The attitude of confrontation and control is quite alien to the relationship, for nature, however difficult some situations may be, is not an adversary to be conquered but an 'other' to be respected. How could the object of God's loving concern come to be regarded as simply an enemy to human beings? Yet our language is still full of bellicose terms, like the 'conquering' of mountains and the 'breaking in' of horses I mentioned before. It is not surprising that some people are turning to Buddhism because it has a gentle attitude to the natural world, while Christianity appears to be locked into its ancient attitudes of domination.[131]

But, as this book maintains, such Christian fixation on power and control over nature 'ain't necessarily so'. In place of these adversarial tactics companionship involves a dialogue of responsiveness to and fro between humanity's interests and nature's. Companionship thus exercised is a fulfilment of the command to love our neighbours as ourselves – our neighbours in this case being our neighbourhood, our environment. Human responsibility is to make a fitting response, and to keep the dialogue going.

I have used the model of companionship because it expresses a sense of 'being in this together' without making some of the impossible demands that, for instance, the more intimate relation of friendship would imply. One could scarcely ask a farmer to be a friend of every sheep, cow or chicken on the farm. But a sense of companionship with the creatures, as opposed to thinking of them as incipient commodities, or even only as stock, seems a possible and fruitful way to behave for their good and the farmer's.

Further, the relationship also serves as a criterion for what kind of action is possible. If all sense of companionship has to be abandoned for a particular course of action to take place, then that action should not be undertaken. One can scarcely be said to *companion* creatures whose lives are confined to crates, or reduced to feeding/egg-laying units; nor could a companion tolerate stressful and inefficient killing at abattoirs. But it is not enough for non-farmers just to be critical of some farming practices. It is up to consumers to companion farmers through the changes, which means, among other things in developed countries, being willing to pay for the cost of humane, companionable farming.

It may be one thing to propose companioning livestock, for they at least have a central nervous system, and their pain is comprehensible. But what of cereals? Surely they are too distant a species from us for companionship to be a reality? Well, it has been done. Barbara McClintock, a Nobel laureate plant geneticist, who perceived that genes may move around in the genome, changing their 'meaning' as they alter their position, wrote passionately on the need to attend to the individual differences between corn plants, 'listening' to them, letting them disclose their own being and efficient processes.

She called this 'a feeling for the organism', and her practice recalls the importance I ascribed earlier to *attention* in relationship, and may be (on the human level with its short span, set categories and many distractions) something like the attention God gives to an individual cheetah and every other creature. For one may hardly be said to companion another when the attention is directed else-where, so that accidental encroachments on, or deliberate exploita-tion of, the companion become possible. For McClintock, even walking over the corn was a form of intrusion.[132]

Such close companionship may not always be possible for a working farmer (although it has a good deal to suggest to gardeners), but even farmers in the midst of European Union regulations and subsidies, concerned with returns per hectare, can *attend* to what makes for the being and well-being of their plants, can work *with* them and the soil in co-operation towards harvest. The rights and wrongs of pesticides or herbicides is too complex an issue to begin to address here. But the conclusion of Rachel Carson's *Silent Spring*, which examined their effects, is still worth quoting. (Her index entry on mammals is arresting as well; it is a list of animals 'killed by ... killed by ... ', naming chemical preparations.)

The 'control of nature' is a phrase conceived in arrogance, born of the Neanderthal Age of biology and philosophy, when it was supposed that nature exists for the convenience of man ... It is our alarming misfortune that so primitive a science has armed itself with the most modern and terrible weapons, and ... has turned them against the earth.[133]

Since DDT was one of the chemicals Carson demonstrated to have wide-ranging and long-lasting effects, it is desolating to observe that although DDT was banned in the US in 1972, that country still manufactures over 18 million kilograms of it a year for export, largely to the Third World.

Ignorance in the Third World of the dangers involved with the use of pesticides is a major problem. A sample of rural workers in Central America shows that they have 11 times as much DDT in their bodies as the average American citizen.[134]

Thus, in the end, although I have deliberately restricted this book to consideration of the natural world, it is not possible to consider companionship between human beings and nature without also raising questions about relationships among human beings themselves. The *Gaia Atlas of Planet Management*, from which the quotation above comes, reports the United Nations estimate of 40,000 people in developing countries killed, and a further million injured, each year as a result of pesticide poisoning. It is not possible to companion plants and animals while ignoring such human inequalities.

Stewardship. Faced with statistics like those just given, and all the other problems of the planet, it may well be thought that something more robust than companionship is needed for action. With that I would agree, but would wish to insist that stewardship without a basic sense of companionship may simply reproduce the attitudes and ways of working which brought about the ecological crisis in the first place.

Stewardship, after all, is a form of management. Indeed in modern translations of Jesus' parables about stewards, the word is translated 'manager'. Management is care over *resources*, and that immediately makes a distinction of kind and not degree between the steward and what is stewarded. Hierarchy is also built into the model, for stewards are 'over' their charges, not 'with' them. This form of relationship, therefore, implies distance and superiority between human beings and all the rest.

In a sense stewardship, even when enlightened by modern knowledge, chastened by past excess and Christianized, is still basically about the manipulation of the natural world, although it substitutes a kindly paternalism for egocentric tyranny.[135]

The notion of managing others for their own good (and our convenience) is too reminiscent of the ideals of Victorian colonialism for comfort, and may carry the same implicit assumptions of superiority over inferior beings, which justifies lordship and mastery rather than companionship.

All of that said, however, it remains the case that the planet is in a mess quite largely of human making, which human intelligence and organization will be required to clear up, in co-operation with each other and other creatures. There are certainly positive aspects to stewardship, and if the negative connotations are noted and guarded against, responsible (fitting into a dialogue of responses) action may be described in terms of this relationship.

A steward has a delegated authority, and Christian stewardship recognizes that 'the earth is the Lord's', and not ours to possess or manipulate at will. If God desires freedom and well-being for creation, then it is the task of human stewards to bring these conditions about. Stewards of the land are 'responsible for its conservation, for its lasting improvement and also for the care of our fellow creatures, its non-human inhabitants'.[136] No steward worthy of the name would allow exploitation of the creatures under her/his care, nor the exhaustion of vital resources. Stewards look to the future as well as the present, and cannot make present profitability in, for instance, clear-felling forests, the sole effective criterion for action with no longer view.

A steward of the whole inhabited world cannot export problems, as Britain exports acid rain, or as the Third World receives known noxious products, and establishments like chemical factories. Apart from the insult and injury to other people involved in that process, for a steward of (finally) the *whole earth* there is nowhere to export the problems to, and they have to be dealt with on the planet. Again, no alert steward would allow a bad situation to become worse through lack of concern or attention, and there are many such situations today, from the hole in the ozone layer over the poles to the accumulation of low-level ozone in city air.

None of this description actually *prescribes* action, since every situation is different, and the estimate of a fitting response always has to be made. When, for instance, does fishing become over-fishing and the depletion or exhaustion of fish-stocks? Because these environmental questions always concern the real world of many interacting possibilities, simple answers are not always available. But just as there are principles concerning the value of the non-human world which guide action, so there are implications in the image of stewardship which make some actions possible and rule out others.

One sensitive theological account of the nature of Christian stewardship for those unused to thinking in that way is given by Douglas Hall in his rendering of imaging God. There stewardship is not control of nature like a human version of the action of an all-powerful God, but is rather the kind of service one would expect from those who follow a Christ who washed his disciples' feet.

> As he represents for us a transvaluation of almost every value our frenetic society teaches us to cherish – the values of possessing things, of achieving mastery, of acquiring eminence among our peers, of winning – so with the same disconcerting logic he pulls us back from the false ambition of being nature's 'lords and possessors' (Hobbes).[137]

What Hall emphasizes instead is the sacrificial element in stewarding: there is a theology of the cross here. At the moment it is non-human creation that is sacrificed for us to fill our supermarkets or provide massive weekend newspapers.

> To be sacrificed that another might live – that is a logic that Christians can perhaps understand; but to end up in the garbage, half-eaten, 'almost new', the victim of built-in obsolescence? (96)

As opposed to all of that there is a sacrificial path of self-denial for the people of God in their use of the natural world. The reverse side of such sacrifice is the preservation of creation. Jesus' death came out of no death-wish; rather, he came that there might be abundant life. The God whom Christianity glorifies glories in creation. In that case:

> To glorify God is to be engaged in a concrete spirituality that refuses to draw marked distinctions between sacred and secular, contemplation and deed, theology and ethics (200).

Stewardship is not, therefore, Hall argues, only the stewardship of souls, traditional in some forms of Christianity, but the preservation of God's valued creation. Finally he concludes that this implies recognizing a spiritual element in matter.

> The corollary of the statement that human being is being-with nature is the recognition that nature, from its side, has a capacity for relatedness (201).

There is mystery in non-human nature which transcends its usefulness to humans and can convey a sense of the presence of God. It behoves human beings, then, to care for it well.

Priesthood is another form of relationship between human beings, the natural world and God which has both positive aspects and limitations. On the positive side, part of the relationship with God will indeed be to share both delight and dismay at what is going on in nature, articulating (as human beings can, but still with our limited human understanding) situations in which we have pleasure and thanksgiving that such things can be, or concern and responsibility where things have gone wrong. Equally, human beings may show reverence towards the natural world, for itself, and as the place of the presence of God. Likewise, their thought and action will be informed by what we believe to be synergy, the flowing together of energies, and co-operation, the interaction of activity, with the God and Father of our Lord Jesus Christ.

In these ways, and to that extent, humans may be priests who, in liturgy, devotion and action, represent articulately the natural world to God and God, in actions expressing freedom and love, to the natural world. There is also a sense in which human beings as priest-representatives of nature have to speak for it in the world:

> The non-human world of animals, plants and inorganic matter cannot represent its own interests; this world needs a voice and champion, now as never before. It is the human race which threatens it, and unless the human being recognizes and acts out his role as representative, the free and willing agent of God's purposes, human attitudes will remain at the level of the manipulative or sentimental, and human influence will be demonic.[138]

What has been problematical in some descriptions of human priestly being-with in the crisis, however, are those which presume that there is *no* relationship between God and the natural world *unless* human beings take on this role. Thus Arthur Peacocke, in spite of insisting on God's presence as lure in a process manner in creation, writes:

> Man's role may be conceived as that of priest of creation as a result of whose activity the sacrament of creation is reverenced; and who, *because he alone is conscious of God, himself and nature*, can mediate between insentient nature and God – for a priest is characterized by activity directed towards God on behalf of others.[139]

What is missing here is the expression of any belief that God is conscious of, indeed relates to, non-human creation as much as human, and therefore does not *depend* on human mediation. It is often implied that God recognizes only human speech, and not that of cheetahs, whales or bats, for instance. That is to project severe limitations on to God, and is part of the hyper-inflation of personal metaphors for God. Further, human beings may represent to God what *human beings* think is going on, but what, on this picture, represents the various views of *non-human nature* on what is going on? All that is to say that our capacity *actually* rather than *intentionally* to represent all of creation is limited, and if God had no direct contact with the natural world divine knowledge would be severely reduced.

Some versions of priesthood as *the* human role in the ecological, then, simply echo in the current situation the ancient belief that God has to do only with humans. Much the same was expressed in the seventeenth century by George Herbert in his poem 'Providence', which is otherwise very sympathetic towards nature.

Beasts fain would sing; birds dittie to their notes;
Trees would be tuning on their native lute
To thy renown; but all their hands and throats
Are brought to Man, while they are lame and mute.

Man is the world's High Priest: he doth present
The sacrifice for all; while they below
Unto the service mutter an assent
Such as springs use that fall, and windes that blow.[140]

What Herbert could not have known, but what is common knowledge today, is that human beings appeared very late on the evolutionary stage. We are homo-come-lately. If the whole course of evolution is condensed into the course of a year, *homo sapiens* makes an appearance around 10pm on 31 December. Who was High Priest during all these aeons, or were they empty of God's love and concern until articulate humanity spared a thought for the environment in prayer? The conclusion must be that the natural world does not *need* us as priests, any more than God *needs* us to uphold the natural world, although it may be a part of human Christian vocation so to act, giving it all a seriousness and enactment within a service of worship.

The presumption involved in believing that there is no connection between God and the natural world unless human beings make it seems to me totally unwarranted and extremely dangerous. If God does not care directly, without mediation, about what happens to felled rain forests, polluted rivers, habitats in drought and habitats in flood, then there is nothing distinctively Christian to bring to the ecological crisis. Of course there is the prayerful, reverential and active role I described earlier as priesthood, while humanity in prayer may bring before God the whole created world. But we are not the pivot on which God and nature depend. *To human beings*, nature has to be recognized to be sacramental before it becomes formally sacramental. But that is not to say that the divine presence began when human beings found resonances in bread and wine, oil and water.

It can only be a good thing that the notion of priesthood takes reverence for, and concern over, the natural world into the heart of worship. But if it is indeed the case, as the Church of England's report *Faith in the Countryside* suggests, that 'the time has come for this description of humankind's relationship with nature to be explored further, and more vigorously accepted',[141] human beings should not confuse that with belief that they are the sole conduit between creation and God.

Co-creator? The question-mark here indicates that while I can see some values in this proposed form of relationship, I am again aware of problems. Its use depends largely on what is understood by God's act of creation. It can fit well with the sense of letting-be, and making room for possibility which I have attributed to God, and on these grounds I have included it. For human beings to be co-creators in *that* sense, they will, for instance, wherever possible, let wilderness be without interference.

> What would the world be, once bereft
> Of wet and wildness? Let them be left
> O let them be left, wildness and wet;
> Long live the weeds and the wilderness yet.[142]

Equally, if less romantically, human beings as co-creators will, wherever possible, let be marvellously evolved ecosystems to explore their own possibilities.

> Man-made ecosystems lack the stability and durability that natural systems acquire from their slow and relentless evolution. We have to live with this mystery and its sobering moral influence. It is no wonder that biologists who have reflected on complexity

regard it as an act of vandalism to upset an ecosystem without good cause for doing so.[143]

If co-creator is understood in this way, letting be, or making room for others to be, it may stand alongside stewardship, suggesting that there are occasions for management and occasions for leaving alone.

For everything there is a season, and a time for every matter under heaven (Eccles.3.1).

The problem is to discern which time it is.

On the other hand, human co-creation modelled on a conception of divine creation as making – or at least as making an initial aim for creatures – has led to some descriptions of the role as revolving around human capacity for creativity. Thus Arthur Peacocke writes:

Man has a derived creativity from God, and all genuine activities of man which attain excellence, and are in accord with God's intentions to build his reign of love (his 'kingdom') may be regarded as man exerting his role as *co-creator* with God.[144]

I warm to the descripton of God's intentions, while human creativity in the arts, in science and technology may indeed be good and beautiful, arousing gratitude that such things may be. I would not resile from any of that, and yet, in the first place, I do not attribute any such creativity to God because that inevitably leads to holding God responsible for natural evil. That perception of ambiguity if divine creativity is emphasized is paralleled, in the second place, by the ambiguity of human creativity, even when the intentions are excellent.

Just how ambiguous human creativity may be becomes clear in this quotation from Piet Schoonenberg in 1964.

God is at work in the growth of plants. He is equally at work in them when we foster their growth by artificial fertilizers. He is present once more in the fabrication of the most synthetic of all fertilizers. Our work likewise does not take anything out of God's hands, for he supports it together with our whole existence.[145]

When Schoonenberg wrote, it was still possible to have an unqualifiedly positive view of fertilizers (given that Rachel Carson was not yet widely read). This human enterprise to increase fertility world-wide would look like creativity building up the kingdom, and it is only with experience and hindsight that the dubious aspect of the whole process becomes clear. I am sure that God was present at 'the fabrication of the most synthetic of fertilizers', but, knowing so much better than human beings what the chemicals were capable of, God may have viewed it all a great deal less optimistically.

Creativity in the arts does not escape ambiguity either, at least in relation to a role of co-creator. The Impressionists may have taught people to 'see' sunlight dancing on water, an enlargement of vision which may be thought of as positive. But Renaissance painters, with a duty to their rich patrons, taught people to 'see' Mary as a rich young woman, fit to be an ornament in aristocratic surroundings, and that creativity may perhaps appear more dubious.

We do not know what ambiguities our present creativity will give rise to. But work on human and trans-species genetics would be a current issue where the ambiguity of the results of creativity is already a contentious issue, and the notion of co-creation in relation to humanly modified creatures has a doubtful ring. Even if the role of co-creator were to be understood modestly, 'as auxiliary and cooperative rather than as dominating and exploitative', in Peacocke's words, it would still have difficulties as a form of self-understanding in associating God with our imperfect works.

If human creativity, even when well-informed and well-intentioned, is steeped in profound and pervasive ambiguity, we can only do the best we can with present understanding and ability, and with rigorous care. Whether 'the best we can' justifies being called 'co-creator' is another question.

Steward, priest, co-creator: these roles work concurrently to prevent any one of them from becoming dominant and leading to a one-sided way of human relating to the natural world. But, as I wrote earlier, companionship is the fundamental from which the others arise, and to which they return. The control involved in stewardship, for instance, is not an end in itself; it exists so that the companionship of humans, nature and God may be enhanced by taking responsibility for the conditions obtaining in the world. On its own, however, it could represent activism without depth.

Priesthood on its own, on the other hand, could be a comfortable ecclesiastical evasion of the practical problems of the crisis if it did not exist alongside stewardship, and if, in the end, it was not directed to the recognition of all creation, human and non-human, as the possible sacrament of divine presence. Co-creation, as I have affirmed it, is the companionship of leaving well alone, not rushing in with stewardship and control where it is possible to let be non-human creation pursuing its own possibilities and its own companionship with God.

A good illustration of these roles in action is the tree-planting eucharist of the African Independent Churches. Once a year, in the rainy season, they set aside 'God's acre' with holes dug ready to receive seedling trees in their sadly denuded countries. Then, in the service, when people have confessed their ecological sins, the bishop sprinkles over the prepared ground holy water of purification and fertility, and soil blessed in the name of Christ. The people receive seedlings as well as wine and bread, and, still within the eucharistic service, plant them.[146] This is part of the liturgy:

Look at the stagnant water
where all the trees were felled.
Without trees the water-holes mourn,
without trees the gullies form,
for the tree roots to hold the soil
are gone!

These friends of ours
give us shade.
They draw the rain clouds,
breathe the moisture of rain.

I, the tree . . . I am your friend.
I know you want wood
for fire:

to cook your food,
to warm yourself against cold.
Use my branches . . .
What I do not need
you can have.

I, the human being,
your closest friend,
have committed a serious offence.
As a *ngozi*, the vengeful spirit,
I destroyed you, our friends.
So the seedlings brought here today
are the 'bodies' of restoration,
a sacrifice to appease
the vengeful spirit.
We plant these seedlings today
as an admission of guilt
laying the *ngozi* to rest,
strengthening our bonds with you,
our tree friends of the heart.

Indeed there were forests,
abundance of rain,
but in our ignorance and greed
we left the land naked.
Like a person in shame
our country is shy
in its nakedness.

Our planting of trees today
is a sign of harmony
between us and creation.
We are reconciled with creation
through the body and blood of Jesus
which brings peace;
he who came to save
all creation.

Part Four

Now and For Ever

Can companionship with God ever end? Does the divine presence with each creature cease as its death makes room for new life? When all life on Earth comes to an end, through human nuclear warfare or the impact of an asteroid, for instance; or when the planet itself is either diffused out into space or compacted into the Big Crunch, will all that has happened be merely a transient diversion in the experience of God?

The only basis for hope beyond death lies in trust in the continuing, eternal love of God. And if this love is for all creatures, not simply for humans, one may hope for eternity in God's presence for them too. Thus there is a sense in which they too are 'saved', the theological word used for divine rescue and transformation of imperfect temporal creation.

However, the whole notion of salvation, what one is saved from, and what saved to, has been differently expressed according to what has been most valued at any time in God's relationship with creation. Within the description I have given, I understand salvation, as far as human beings are concerned, to mean the discovery that a relationship with God already exists; that one is already befriended, judged, forgiven; that a continuing mutual relationship has been made possible by God's initiative, within which human belief and action may respond to divine encouragement, reproof or consolation; and that this synergy or concurrence is always possible between the human and the divine.[1]

For Christians, Jesus is the one who in life made such concurrence visible and effective, and in death showed that nothing could separate us from the love of God. Jesus enacted for those with eyes to see what God is *always* like. Salvation, therefore, is not some new divine initiative after creation unfortunately fell from grace, but rather is the always-present possibility for everyone of concurrence with God rescuing and transforming human being and doing from a pointlessness of existence here and now.

What I have just been describing has been a human creature's view of creation/salvation. Yet one of the limitations of such a human account is that it may easily become egocentric, concerning what salvation does for me – *my* rescue, *my* transformation – even if one may be thankful to God for it. However important individual salvation is to the individual, it should be possible to raise our eyes from our own concerns to ask what *God* finds in creation worthy of eternity, and what *God* derives from these relationships.

The key, I suggest, is to be found in the notion of concurrence. God maintains relationship with all at all times. For human beings there are cues to this in church and Bible, in varieties of experience, and in the possibilities of freedom and love. But it always remains possible that people may simply concentrate on their own comfort and advancement, some of the time at least, doing nothing to enlarge freedom and love, making no response to Christ, and, in short, not concurring with God. Judgment falls on such times, which in their divorce from God and the divine purposes are not worthy of being saved, and so are dismissed to oblivion and non-being.

But times when freedom is exercised in love, moments of concurrence with God's desire for creation, are saved and remain in God's eternal presence. This interprets salvation in terms of *moments*, and their actors, which please God, rather than *people* who are pleasing from beginning to end. Therefore, instead of people being, so to speak, 100% 'in' or 'out' of salvation and eternity, only those parts of lives which please God, which bear the desired fruit from the seed of possibility, are saved. Whatever runs with God now (concurrence), whatever works with God now (synergy, cooperation), is what God may be said to desire from creation now and for ever.

It is possible to extend the same notion of concurrence to the natural world as well, only here it does not have the moral cast which is part of human possibility. Creaturely freedom in the use of possibility, creaturely enjoyment of life and flourishing in conditions which enhance its relationships are the moments of God's joy in creation, and its concurrence with divine desire. Whatever in non-human nature, or in the relationships between human beings and non-human beings, concurs with God, becomes part of God's positive experience, which is eternal, and hence cannot be lost. Again, what does not concur is relegated to non-being, which is its proper status.

Eternity is not a place where creatures can develop, for development requires space and time. Eternity, on the other hand, simply *is* (and is thus impossible to speak of, except in pictures). What is eternal, therefore, is what at some moment in time *is*, with all that is negative, unfree, unloving sifted from it, and what is positive transformed into part of a new and satisfying whole. Quite possibly this new whole may not have the linear shape historians give to an account in time. It may be more like the multiplicity of a stream of consciousness as described by the protagonist in Penelope Lively's *Moon Tiger*:

> I've always thought a kaleidoscopic view might be an interesting heresy. Shake the tube and see what comes out. Chronology irritates me. There is no chronology inside my head. I am composed of a myriad Claudias who spin and mix and part like sparks of sunlight on water; . . . there is no sequence, everything happens at once.[2]

I have already concurred with Bergson's description of time in the universe as retardation, so that everything does not happen at once, while space equally spreads things out. Conversely, eternity, with no time or space, could have this kind of kaleidoscopic simultaneity.

The human worry may be whether I shall remain 'myself' in all this. We are so attached to ourselves, and have such difficulty in thinking of God as anything more than a perfect person, so that we may relate to God as person to person. But the important thing about creation is not who we are on our own, but rather what of God's desire for creation has been fulfilled in our relationships. So what is preserved in eternity is not so much a purified self, which bears only a partial relationship to how we were, as the self we were in all the moments of concurrence, because that self will be able to relate with joy to all the other moments and beings gathered up as a result of teleology now!

There are difficulties in this picture, as there are in any attempt to speak of eternity, especially when it begins to be worked out in detail. Some lives have had much more chance of freedom and love than others, for instance, but if God knows all the conditions, God may be trusted to discern what humans could not judge. But this version does avoid some difficulties implicit in some other pictures. Would a lion, for instance, a carnivore, still be a lion if it were able to lie down with a lamb? Isaiah's vision requires considerable redesigning of animals and plants from their earthly existence. The lion's experience as lion, hunting on the savannahs, is lost.

But if whatever in that experience pleased or concurred with God were saved, then that particular value, as it was as part of creation and not in another state beyond it, becomes eternal. This is certainly different from the biblical picture which describes initial harmony (Genesis) regained in Isaiah's peaceable kingdom. But that simply omits that much more mixed earthly experience from the whole equation, as if it had no value to God. In trying to think of British parallels to Isaiah's lion and lamb I thought of foxes and rabbits. Thinking of rabbits I thought that there could be no procreation in Isaiah's kingdom. But then all the pleasure at earthly babies, at spindly fawns, at exact miniature grass snakes emerging from their eggs would be lost. The only way to understand the saving of all that is worth saving in creation is to understand the kingdom of God as a kaleidoscope of what *happens* within time, of what makes creation worthwhile now to God. Therefore teleology is always now; what happens now either is or is not of the kingdom.

Concurrence with God, then, holds the key, for what God has concurred in cannot be lost. Since in the natural world this concurrence is, in part, made possible by the conditions of life, there is all the more reason for human beings to be concerned with these conditions where they remove freedom or utterly constrict possibility. The greatest thing human beings can do for non-human beings is to make the conditions for concurrence possible, thus themselves concurring with God. Here, now (and for ever) is what Kathy Galloway has called 'God's graceful moment':

> Morning opens wide before us
> Like a door into the light.
> Just beyond, the day lies waiting
> Ready to throw off the night,
> And we stand upon its threshold
> Poised to turn and take its flight.

> We receive God's graceful moment
> While the day is fresh and still,
> Ours to choose how we will greet it,
> Ours to make it what we will.
> Here is given perfect freedom
> Every hope in love to fulfil.[3]

If all life, all creation, encounters such continuous grace-full possibility, then the response is quite properly that invoked in many psalms, the praise of God. Stewardship and co-creation become fulfilled in enabling that praise, priesthood articulates it, and companionship shares in it with all creation. In his commentary on Psalm 150, Artur Weiser succinctly sums up the belief which it expresses: 'In praising God the meaning of the world is fulfilled.'[4]

There is no difference in such psalms between human beings and non-human beings; they are caught up together in a response of praise to God for their being. In the poem of Herbert's which I quoted earlier, birds and beasts and trees are mute, and so need humanity to give them a voice. However, for the Psalmist, everything in its own way can praise:

> Praise the Lord from the earth
> you sea monsters and all deeps,

fire and hail, snow and frost,
stormy wind fulfilling his command!

Mountains and all hills,
fruit trees and all cedars!
Wild animals and all cattle,
creeping things and flying birds (Ps. 148.7–10).

There is an order in this psalm which recurs in the Benedicite, the song of blessing from the three young men in the fiery furnace in the apocryphal addition to the book of Daniel. After blessing God, the call to bless begins with the inhabitants of the heavens, moves to earth, land, sea and weather with all their creatures, then to humanity in general, then to Israel, then finally to the three in the furnace. Following this pattern, my personal, individual praise is only part of a whole response from the creation of which I am a part. It is the fitting response of the whole created world to its Creator.

Although the Psalmist believed that God had made an orderly creation whose process was divinely commanded, his holistic vision of a response of praise from every creature can still be rendered in terms of a creation which has come into being through the letting-be of possibility. Non-human creation may or may not be aware of God, but in the activity of exploring, adapting, finding out the possibilities of being and doing in whatever range is open to them, their attachment to life is a form of praise to the one who let it be. Humans have special roles, since they have special abilities, but what they do also may praise God by concurring in graceful possibilities of freedom and love, or it may magnify the self, as if that self were all its own work and the final good.

Traditional pictures of heaven have often included choirs singing the praises of God for ever and ever. Understandably, that picture has not appealed to everyone. It has also appeared somewhat narcissistic of God to enjoy that. But if the eternal praise of God happens through a kaleidoscope of times 'when the meaning of the world is fulfilled' in Weiser's phrase, or, in other words, if eternity is filled with rescued and transformed transient creaturely being and doing which pleases God, from the cosmological beginning of creation to its end, then heaven will be a place of infinite and eternal interest and joy.

All your works shall give thanks to you, O Lord;
and all your faithful shall bless you (Ps.145.10).

Notes

Introduction: The Scope of the Study

1. Lewis Thomas, cited without reference in *The Gaia Atlas of Planet Management*, revised ed., ed N. Myers, Gaia Books Ltd 1994.
2. *The Gaia Atlas of Planet Management* (n.1) gives an exhaustive account.
3. The best known of these criticisms, which makes 1967 a watershed year for the apprehension of the ecological crisis as a religious problem, is Lynn White, 'The Historical Roots of our Ecologic Crisis', *Science* 155, 1967, 1203–7.
4. *Carmina Gadelica* I, 279. *The Celtic Vision*, ed. E. de Waal, Darton, Longman and Todd 1988, 61.
5. Edwin Muir, 'The Fall', *Collected Poems*, Faber and Faber 1976 (1960), 69.
6. N. MacCaig, 'No end, no beginning', *Collected Poems*, Chatto and Windus 1985, 206.
7. N. Cooper, 'Wildlife Conservation in Churchyards: A Case Study in Ethical Judgments', *Biodiversity and Conservation* 4, 1995, 919.
8. E. Doogue, 'Poverty's Toll: UN Summit for Social Development', *One World* 205, May 1995, 4.
9. J. Polkinghorne, *Science and Creation*, SPCK 1988, 25.
10. E. Brunner, *The Christian Doctrine of Creation and Redemption*, Lutterworth Press 1952, 39–42.
11. I. Ball, 'Sing an Old-fashioned Song', *The Earth Beneath: A Critical Guide to Green Theology*, ed. I. Ball, M. Goodall, C. Palmer and J. Reader, SPCK 1992, 125.

Part One: Creation as Possibility and Freedom

1. A.N. Wilson, *A Bottle in the Smoke*, Penguin Books 1992, 169.
2. J. Macquarrie, *Principles of Christian Theology*, SCM Press 1966, 195.
3. M. Heidegger, *Essence of Language*, Gesamtausgabe 12, Klostermann 1975, 187.

4. J. Llewellyn, *The Middle Voice of Ecological Conscience*, Macmillan 1991, 86.

5. Ibid., 211.

6. That history may be found in e.g. T. Ferris, *Coming of Age in the Milky Way*, The Bodley Head 1989.

7. K.R. Popper, *A World of Propensities*, Thoemmes 1990, 12.

8. P. Davies and J. Gribbin, *The Matter Myth*, Viking Penguin Books 1991, 21.

9. Popper, *A World of Propensities*, 12. Further references to this book are given in brackets in the text.

10. R.F. Holland, *Against Empiricism: On Education, Epistemology and Value*, Blackwell 1980, 218.

11. H. Bergson, *The Creative Mind. An Introduction to Metaphysics*, The Wisdom Library nd, 100f.

12. C. Isham, 'Quantum Theories of the Creation of the Universe', in *Interpreting the Universe as Creation*, in V. Brümmer (ed.), Kok Pharos 1991, 53ff.

13. S. Hawking, *A Brief History of Time*, Bantam Books 1988, 141.

14. J. Rogerson, *Genesis 1–11*, JSOT Press 1991, 61.

15. J. Calvin, *Institutes of the Christian Religion*, Book 1.5.2.

16. M. Munitz, *The Mystery of Existence*, New York University Press 1974, 105.

17. K. Ferguson, *The Fire in the Equations: Science, Religion and the Search for God*, Bantam Books 1995, 128.

18. J.W.B. Drees, *Beyond the Big Bang; Quantum Cosmologies and God*, Open Court 1990, 99.

19. P. Davies, *The Mind of God: Science and the Search for Ultimate Meaning*, Simon and Schuster 1992, 67.

20. Ibid., 68.

21. Drees, *Beyond the Big Bang* (n.18), 97, citing C. Isham, 'Creation of the Universe as a Quantum Problem', in *Physics, Philosophy and Theology*, ed. R. Russell, W. Stoeger and G. Coyne, Vatican Observatory/University of Notre Dame Press 1988, 401.

22. R. Page, *Ambiguity and the Presence of God*, SCM Press 1985, 35–40.

23. J. Polkinghorne, *Reason and Reality*, SPCK 1991, 57.

24. Davies, *The Mind of God* (n.19), 81.

25. R. Harré, *Laws of Nature*, Duckworth 1993, 34 (further references to this book are given in brackets in the text).

26. Polkinghorne, *Reason and Reality* (n.24), 23.

27. Cf. P. Clayton, *Explanation from Physics to Theology: An Essay in Rationality and Religion*, Yale University Press 1989.

28. Polkinghorne, *Reason and Reality* (n.24), 40 (further references to this book are given in the text).

29. I. Prigogine and I. Stengers, *Order out of Chaos: Man's New Dialogue with Nature*, Flamingo 1984, 78.

30. Ibid., xxvii.

31. J. Ray, *The Wisdom of God as Manifested in the Works of the Creation*, 1691.

32. P. Marshall, *Nature's Web: An Exploration of Ecological Thinking*, Simon and Schuster 1992, 209.

33. W. Paley, *Natural Theology; or The Evidences of the Existence and Attributes of the Deity, collected from the Appearances of Nature*, F.C.N. Rivington et al.1815, 317f.

34. Brunner, *Christian Doctrine of Creation* (n.10), 18.

35. Ibid., 17.

36. Paley, *Evidences* (n.34), 456.

Part Two: Creation as Presence and Relationship

1. G.Steiner, *Heidegger*, Fontana Books 1978, 81.

2. J. Moltmann, *God in Creation. An Ecological Doctrine of Creation*, SCM Press 1985, 149.

3. T. Berry, with T. Clarke, *Befriending the Earth*, Twenty-Third Publications 1991, 19.

4. Starhawk, *The Spiral Dance: A Rebirth of the Ancient Religion of the Great Goddess*, Harper and Row 1979, 77f.

5. N. Pittenger, *Process Thought and Christian Faith*, Nisbet 1968, 40.

6. Cf. C. Birch, *On Purpose*, New South Wales University Press 1990; A. Peacocke, *Creation and the World of Science*, Clarendon Press 1979; I. Barbour, *Religion in an Age of Science*, SCM Press 1990.

7. C. Hartshorne, *A Natural Theology for our Time*, Open Court 1967, 58.

8. J. B. Cobb and D. R. Griffin, *Process Theology: an Introductory Exposition*, Westminster Press 1977, 28.

9. D. Pailin, *God and the Processes of Reality: Foundations of a Credible Theism*, Routledge 1989, 140.

10. P.T. Geach, *Providence and Evil*, Cambridge University Press 1977, 70f.

11. K. Ward, *Rational Theology and the Creativity of God*, Blackwell 1982, 115.
12. Ibid.
13. Moltmann, *God in Creation* (n.2), 87. Cf. id., *The Trinity and the Kingdom of God*, SCM Press 1981, 111.
14. H. Bergson, *The Creative Mind*, The Wisdom Library, nd, 93.
15. K. Rahner, 'Christology Today', in K. Rahner and W. Thüsing, *A New Christology*, Burns and Oates 1980, 15.
16. Cf. G. Gutierrez, *A Theology of Liberation*, SCM Press 1974, [2]1988.
17. K. Ward, *Rational Theology and the Creativity of God*, Blackwell 1982, 209.
18. J. Grimshaw, 'The Idea of a Female Ethic', in *A Companion to Ethics*, ed. P. Singer, Blackwell 1993, 495.
19. S. McFague, *The Body of God: An Ecological Theology*, SCM Press 1993, 49f.
20. Moltmann, *God in Creation* (n.2), 14.
21. S.Maitland, *A Big-enough God: Artful Theology*, Mowbray 1995, 64.
22. R. Page, *The Incarnation of Freedom and Love*, SCM Press 1991.
23. P.T. Geach, *Providence and Evil*, Cambridge University Press 1977, 65.
24. E. Brunner, *The Christian Doctrine of Creation and Redemption*, Lutterworth Press 1952, 14.
25. On the strengths and weaknesses of voluntaristic and emanationist accounts of creation, see Moltmann, *God in Creation* (n.2), 79–86.
26. Brunner, *The Christian Doctrine of Creation* (n.24), 18.
27. Ibid., 175.
28. E.P Odum, *Ecology*, Holt, Rinehart and Winston 1975, 1.
29. V. Blackmore and A. Page, *Evolution: The Great Debate*, Lion Publishing 1989, 97.
30. A. Peacocke, *Creation and the World of Science*, Clarendon Press 1979, 212.
31. A. Peacocke, *Theology for a Scientific Age*, Blackwell 1990, 109.
32. K. Ferguson, *The Fire in the Equations: Science, Religion and the Search for God*, Bantam Books 1995, 164.
33. This is certainly the argument favoured by J. Barrow and F. Tipler, *The Anthropic Cosmological Principle*, Oxford University Press 1986.
34. Ferguson, *The Fire in the Equations* (n.2), 166.
35. S. Hawking, *A Brief History of Time*, Bantam Books 1988, 133.
36. Ferguson, *The Fire in the Equations* (n.2), 176. On the Higgs boson cf. A.

Daniels, 'Point of Creation', *Edit*, University of Edinburgh Magazine, Winter 1994, 18–20.

37. S.J. Gould, *The Flamingo's Smile: Reflections in Natural History*, Penguin Books 1987, 395.

38. M. Midgley, *Science as Salvation: A Modern Myth and Its Meaning*, Routledge 1992, 202.

39. L. Thomas, *Lives of a Cell: Notes of a Biology Watcher*, Futura Publications 1974, 145f.

40. J. Wheeler, 'Law without Law', in *Quantum Mechanics and Measurement*, ed. J. Wheeler and W. Zurek, Princeton University Press 1983, 209.

41. For the Uncertainty Principle, and the Copenhagen Interpretation based upon it, cf. H. Pagels, 'Uncertainty and Complementarity', *The World Treasury of Physics, Astronomy and Mathematics*, ed. T. Ferris, Little, Brown and Company 1991, 97–110.

42. J. Wheeler, 'Information, Physics, Quantum: The Search for Links', cited without further reference by P. Davies and J. Gribbin, *The Matter Myth: Towards Twenty-First Century Science*, Viking 1991, 300f.

43. S.J. Gould, *Wonderful Life: The Burgess Shale and the Nature of History*, Penguin Books 1989, 51.

44. Ibid.

45. Ibid.

Part Three: The Companioned World

1. T. Pratchett and N. Gaiman, *Good Omens*, Corgi Books 1991.

2. R. Dawkins, *The Selfish Gene*, Oxford University Press 1976, 2.

3. E. Wilson, *Sociobiology: The New Synthesis*, Harvard University Press 1975, 3.

4. M. Midgley, *Evolution as a Religion: Strange Shapes and Stranger Fears*, Methuen 1985, 127.

5. N. Eldredge, *The Miner's Canary*, Prentice Hall 1991, 146.

6. Eldredge, *The Miner's Canary* (n.5), 31.

7. Ibid.

8. S. Oyama, *The Ontogeny of Information*, Cambridge University Press 1985, 72.

9. Ibid., 71.

10. Eldredge, *The Miner's Canary* (n.5), 11.

11. R. Dawkins, *The Blind Watchmaker*, Penguin Books 1990, 136. Author's emphasis.
12. On the difficulties of perceiving providence in history, see e.g. Van Harvey, *The Historian and the Believer*, SCM Press 1967.
13. Oyama, *Ontogeny of Information* (n.8), 71.
14. Cf. L. Stone, *The Causes of the English Revolution*, Routledge, Kegan Paul 1972.
15. M. Midgley, *Science as Salvation: A Modern Myth and Its Meaning*, Routledge 1972, 51. Cf. this review of Dawkins' latest book, *River out of Eden*, Weidenfeld and Nicholson 1995: 'Like many others Dawkins seems to equate strong science with the calculable predictability of the billiards table, and so needs to envisage living systems as being composed of fully discrete, particulate units of selection. He has no time for fuzzy boundaries, complex feedbacks and the huge significance of serendipitous processes, and so espouses a worldview that leads straight to an overemphasis on competition and centralized power' (A. Rayner, 'Limited Science', *Resurgence* 173, Nov./Dec. 1995, 54).
16. R.F. Holland, *Against Empiricism: On Education, Epistemology and Value*, Blackwell 1980, 225.
17. J. Bowker, *Is God a Virus?*, SPCK 1995, 98.
18. P. Clayton, *Explanation from Physics to Theology: An Essay in Rationality and Religion*, Yale University Press 1989, 34.
19. Bowker, *Is God a Virus?* (n.17), 99.
20. Ibid., 106, citing W.R. Ashby, *An Introduction to Cybernetics*, London 1956, 3.
21. *Man and Nature*, ed. H. Montefiore, Collins 1975, 41.
22. R.P. Meye, 'Invitation to Wonder: Towards a Theology of Nature', in *Tending the Garden*, ed. W. Granberg-Michaelson, Eerdmans 1987, 35.
23. E. Brunner, *The Christian Doctrine of Creation and Redemption*, Lutterworth Press 1952, 40.
24. Meye, 'Invitation to Wonder' (n.22), 36.
25. P. Fiddes, *The Creative Suffering of God*, Clarendon Press 1988, 221.
26. A good selection of quotations on this subject is assembled by A. Linzey, *Animal Rights*, SCM Press 1976.
27. *Man and Nature* (n.21), 36.
28. Brunner, *Christian Doctrine of Creation* (n.23), 17.

29. Letter to Asa Grey, *The Life and Letters of Charles Darwin*, ed. Francis Darwin, John Murray 1888, II, 105.
30. Cited without reference in S.J. Gould, 'Non-moral Nature', in *The Sacred Beetle and other great essays in science*, ed. M. Gardner, Oxford University Press, revised edition 1985, 45.
31. K. Ward, *Rational Theology and the Creativity of God*, Blackwell 1982, 114.
32. P.T. Geach, *Providence and Evil*, Cambridge University Press 1977, 77.
33. Ibid.
34. D. Hume, *Dialogues concerning Natural Religion*, Hafner Publishing House 1969, 77.
35. Ibid., 79.
36. A.O. Lovejoy, *The Great Chain of Being*, Harvard University Press 1936, 221.
37. H. Rolston III, *Environmental Ethics: Duties to and Values in the Natural World*, Temple University Press 1988, 173.
38. B. Hebblethwaite, *Evil, Suffering and Religion*, Sheldon Press 1976, 77.
39. A. Peacocke, *Creation and the World of Science*, Clarendon Press 1979, 166.
40. Brunner, *Christian Doctrine of Creation* (n.23), 13.
41. J. Dickie, *The Organism of Christian Truth*, James Clark 1930, 43.
42. A. Farrer, *Love Almighty and Ills Unlimited*, Collins 1962, 99.
43. Ibid., 103.
44. A. Farrer, *A Science of God?*, Geoffrey Bles 1966, 76.
45. J. Cobb and D. Griffin, *Process Theology: An Introductory Exposition*, Westminster Press 1976, 52.
46. Ibid., 53.
47. Farrer, *A Science of God?* (n.44), 88.
48. C. Hartshorne, *The Logic of Perfection*, Open Court 1962, 204.
49. D. Pailin, *God and the Processes of Reality*, Routledge 1989, 140.
50. S.M. Stanley, *Extinction*, Scientific American Library 1987, 11.
51. C. Raven, *Natural Religion and Christian Theology*, Cambridge University Press 1953, 127.
52. L. White, 'The Historical Roots of our Ecologic Crisis,' *Science* 155, March 1967.
53. K. Tester, *Animals and Society: The Humanity of Animal Rights*, Routledge 1991, 195.

54. R. Grove-White, 'Human Identity and the Environmental Crisis,' in *The Earth Beneath: A Critical Guide to Green Theology*, ed. I. Ball, M. Goodall, C. Palmer and J. Reader, SPCK 1992, 16f. Further references to this article are in brackets in the text.

55. H. Küng, *Global Responsibility: In Search of a New World Ethic*, SCM Press 1991, 91.

56. J. Porritt, 'Let the Green Spirit Live', in *The Green Fuse*, ed. J. Button, Quartet Books 1990, 142. The quotation from N. Evernden, *Natural Alien – Humankind and the Environment*, is given without further reference.

57. G. Beer, *Darwin's Plots: Evolutionary Narrative in Darwin, George Eliot and Nineteenth-Century Fiction*, Ark Paperbacks 1985, 13.

58. P. Singer, *Animal Liberation*, Jonathan Cape 1990.

59. Grove-White, 'Human Identity' (n.54), 13.

60. G. von Rad, *Genesis*, SCM Press 1963, 56.

61. S. McFague, *The Body of God: An Ecological Theology*, SCM Press 1993, 16.

62. H.C.B. Moule, *Outline of Christian Doctrine*, Hodder and Stoughton 1905, 157f.

63. K. Barth, *Church Dogmatics*, III.1, T. and T. Clark 1958, 84.

64. Brunner, *The Christian Doctrine of Creation* (n.23), 56.

65. Ibid., 59.

66. D. J. Hall, *Imaging God: Dominion as Stewardship*, Eerdmans, 1986.

67. von Rad, *Genesis* (n.60), 57.

68. J. C. L. Gibson, *Genesis*, Vol 1, St Andrew Press 1981, 73.

69. J. Rogerson, *Genesis 1–11*, JSOT Press 1991, 127.

70. Hall, *Imaging God* (n.66), 127.

71. Barth, *Church Dogmatics*, III.3, T. and T. Clark 1961, 94.

72. R. Page, *The Incarnation of Freedom and Love*, SCM Press 1991, 53-6.

73. L. Larkin, 'Douglas John Hall – The Stewardship Symbol and the Image of God', *Theology in Green*, Issue 7, July 1993, 19.

74. Cf. the quotation from J. Dickie cited above: *Natural Evil* (n.41).

75. A. Pope, *Essay on Man*, Ep.ii,1,15.

76. *In God's Image: Reflections on Identity, Human Wholeness and the Authority of Scripture*, ed. J. Crawford and M. Kinnamon, World Council of Churches 1983, 69f.

77. J. B. McDaniel, *With Roots and Wings: Christianity in an Age of Ecology and Dialogue*, Orbis Books 1995, 92.

78. I. Bradley, *God is Green*, Darton, Longman and Todd 1990, 1.

79. McDaniel, *With Roots and Wings* (n.77), 91.

80. *Gaudium et Spes* II.34, cf. *Populorum Progressio* I.22. As late as 1981 *Laborem Exercens* used the text 'subdue the earth' to say that all natural resources existed for human ends.

81. J. Mouroux, *The Meaning of Man*, Sheed and Ward 1948, 28.

82. D. Cupitt, 'Natural Evil', in *Man and Nature* (n.21), 118.

83. von Rad, *Genesis* (n.60), 58.

84. 'God in Nature and History', Appendix for *Workbook for the Fourth Assembly*, World Council of Churches 1968, 22.

85. White, 'The Historical Roots of our Ecologic Crisis' (n.52), 1203–7.

86. G. Coles, 'Past, Present and Future: The Science of Environmental Archaeology', *Edit*, University of Edinburgh Magazine, Issue 3, Winter 1992/3, 25.

87. J. Black, *The Dominion of Man*, Edinburgh University Press 1970, 121.

88. J. McPhee, *The Control of Nature*, Pimlico 1991.

89. Ibid., 94.

90. *Our Common Future*, The World Commission on Environment and Development, Oxford University Press 1987, 8.

91. J. Calvin, *Commentaries on the First Book of Moses, called Genesis*, Calvin Translation Society 1847, 96.

92. Cf. A. Leopold, *The Sand County Almanac* (1949), Oxford University Press 1968; A. Naess, *Ecology, Community and Lifestyle: Outline of an Ecosophy*, Cambridge University Press 1989.

93. E.g. J. Nash, *Loving Nature: Ecological Integrity and Christian Responsibility*, Abingdon Press 1991.

94. B. Devall and G. Sessions, *Deep Ecology: Living as if Nature Mattered*, Peregrine Smith Books 1985, 70.

95. P. Marshall, *Nature's Web: an Exploration of Ecological Thinking*, Simon and Schuster 1992, 419.

96. B. Almond, 'Rights', in *A Companion to Ethics*, ed. P. Singer, Blackwell 1993, 262.

97. Ibid., 266.

98. Marshall, *Nature's Web* (n.95), 434.

99. Nash, *Loving Nature* (n.93), 169–76.

100. Ibid., 175.

101. Ibid., 186ff.

102. H.R. Niebuhr, *The Responsible Self: An Essay in Christian Moral Philosophy*, Harper and Row 1963.

103. Nash, *Loving Nature* (n.93), 170.

104. Niebuhr, *Responsible Self* (n.102), 56.
105. Ibid., 61.
106. J.Gustafson and J. Laney (eds.), Introduction to *On Being Responsible: Issues in Personal Ethics*, SCM Press 1968, 11.
107. Niebuhr, *Responsible Self* (n.102), 79.
108. Ibid., p.81
109. Ibid.
110. Now P. Singer, *Animal Liberation*, Jonathan Cape 1990.
111. Cf. P. Ehrlich, *The Machinery of Nature: The Living World Around Us and How It Works*, Simon and Schuster 1986.
112. H. Rolston, *Environmental Ethics: Duties to and Values in the Natural World*, Temple University Press 1988, 108.
113. Ibid., 109.
114. Ibid., 173.
115. Nash, *Loving Nature* (n.93), 177.
116. T.J. Jacob, 'Global Response to HIV Aids: The Churches' Responsibility', unpublished paper, 12.
117. C. Birch, *On Purpose*, New South Wales University Press 1990, 133.
118. Nash, *Loving Nature* (n.93), 182.
119. Ibid.
120. H. Daly and J. Cobb, *For the Common Good: Redirecting the Economy towards Community, the Environment and a Sustainable Future*, Beacon Press 1989, 378.
121. Nash, *Loving Nature* (n.93), 181.
122. S. Clark, *How to Think about the Earth: Philosophical and Theological Models for Ecology*, Mowbray 1993, 115.
123. J. Cobb, *Is It Too Late? A Theology of Ecology*, Bruce 1972, 55.
124. Nash, *Loving Nature* (n.93), 178.
125. Cf.n.101.
126. Clark, *How to Think about the Earth* (n.122), 115.
127. R. Carson, *Silent Spring*, Penguin Books 1965.
128. This is described in greater detail in my *Ambiguity and the Presence of God*, SCM Press 1985, 124f.
129. G. Hendry, *Theology of Nature*, Westminster Press 1980, 17.
130. R. Page, 'The Earth is the Lord's', in *While the Earth Endures*, ed. C. Somerville, Society, Religion and Technology Project, Church of Scotland 1986, 12.
131. E.g. J. Macy, 'Faith and Ecology', in *The Green Fuse* (n.56), 97–108.

132. A feminist account of McClintock's work appears in E.F. Kelly, *Reflections on Gender and Science*, Yale University Press 1985.

133. Carson, *Silent Spring* (n.127), 125.

134. *The Gaia Atlas of Planet Management*, Revised and extended edition, Gen.ed. N. Myers, Gaia Books 1994, 121.

135. R. Page, 'The Fellowship of all Creation', *Theology in Green*, Issue 7, July 1993. 4.

136. R. Attfield, *The Ethic of Environmental Concern*, Blackwell 1983, 45.

137. D.J. Hall, *Imaging God* (n.66), 193. Further references to this book are in brackets in the text.

138. *Faith in the Countryside: Report of the Archbishop's Commission on Rural Areas*, Churchman Publishing 1990, 15.

139. Peacocke, *Creation and the World of Science* (n.39), 296. My emphasis.

140. 'Providence', *The Poems of George Herbert*, Oxford University Press 1961, 107.

141. *Faith in the Countryside* (n.138), 15.

142. G. Manley Hopkins, 'Inversnaid', in *The Faber Book of Modern Verse*, Faber and Faber 1960, 62.

143. E. Ashby, *Reconciling Man and the Environment*, Oxford University Press 1978, 84.

144. Peacocke, *Creation and the World of Science* (n.39), 307.

145. P. Schoonenberg, *God's World in the Making*, Duquesne University Press 1964, 163.

146. M.L. Daniel, 'African Independent Churches Face the Challenge of Environmental Ethics', unpublished paper for a conference on *The Role of Christianity in Development, Peace and Reconstruction*, Malawi 1993.

Part Four: Now and For Ever

1. This understanding of salvation is expressed at greater length in my *The Incarnation of Freedom and Love*, SCM Press 1991.

2. P. Lively, *Moon Tiger*, Penguin Books 1988, 2.

3. K. Galloway, *Love Burning Deep: Poems and Lyrics*, SPCK 1993, 4.

4. A. Weiser, *The Psalms*, SCM Press 1962, 841.

Index of Modern Authors